the
Gift
of
Easter

the Gift of
Easter

compiled and edited
by Floyd Thatcher

WORD BOOKS, Publisher
Waco, Texas

IN APPRECIATION

for each of my friends

who are a part of this book

and have made it possible

through their

generous contributions

CONTENTS

Contents

INTRODUCTION

THIS BOOK CAME INTO MY LIFE at a very good time. I have been going through one of those periods of grayness when the Jesus story seems like a shadowy myth from the "dawn of the Christian era." God and purpose seemed vague, and I was losing track of what was important and what was peripheral in life.

But as I began to read these statements, affirmations, biblical exegeses and living witnesses regarding the meaning of Easter, my faith stirred again. I saw once more that with all of the agony of confessing one's sins and coming to Jesus Christ as Lord and Savior, that his is the only hope and the only way I know worth betting one's life on.

The authors are from different places geographically —one is an Englishman, one a Texan—as well as theologically and socially. But there is a common thread of hope and clarity about the centrality and essential nature of what the cross and resurrection mean—or can mean—in the lives of individuals and the life of the Church.

Having known several of the contributors personally for some time, I know that many of their words about Easter are distilled from the tears of tragedy and frustration. At least two have lost children through those sudden and mystifying illnesses which can strike a

Introduction

Christian family and, like a lightening bolt, destroy happiness and belief. The kind of faith which is hammered out on the anvils of the pain, frustration, and doubt through facing life on its outer edges—this kind of faith is worth examining.

Some of the statements you are about to read come from years of studying the basic documents of the faith. But somehow more convincing to me is the fact that the authors I know have been living in the caldron of life, working and dying with real people.

I am happy to introduce this book and join the authors in wishing for you a blessed Easter and a new life in Christ.

Keith Miller

Watch and Pray

John R. W. Stott

Watch and pray that you may not enter into temptation, the spirit indeed is willing, but the flesh is weak (Mark 14:38).

In Looking at the "Real Jesus" over against a variety of popular caricatures, we must examine that remarkable episode which was vividly described by Matthew, Mark, and Luke: the agony of Jesus in the Garden of Gethsemane. Here is one of the most touching and moving stories in all literature.

Early in the evening Jesus had enjoyed supper in the Upper Room in an atmosphere of warmth and fellowship with men he had come to love dearly. But now, in the chill and darkness of the night, he wrestled with the black agony of his soul, "My soul is very sorrowful, even to death." Yes, he was about to be sold out by one of the twelve he had trusted; torturous death on the cross was just hours away. In simple yet poignant phrases Mark describes the Master's struggle in the fourteenth chapter of his Gospel. These are indeed climactic moments in the history of the human race.

There are two immediate lessons we can learn from this garden scene. First, we become acutely aware of *the humanity of Jesus*. In Gethsemane, Jesus felt deep human emotions of distress and sorrow and shrank with all his being from death on the cross. The Gospel writers tell us he agonized in prayer "with strong cries and tears" and he sweated so profusely that his sweat fell from him like great drops of blood.

The story also makes it clear that Jesus had a will of his own, so that he could distinguish it from and surrender it to the will of his Father. Indeed, this was no ethereal Jesus, remote from human temptation, grief, and pain.

It is quite understandable that this incident has been a theological battleground from the beginning. On the one hand, the Arians (who denied the deity of Jesus) used this story to bolster up their case. On the other, orthodox Christians used it against the Docetists who taught that Jesus was not a real man but only a phantom. The same argument goes on today. We have to contend both for the deity of Jesus (against those who try to reduce him to mere manhood) and for his real tear-sweat-blood humanity (against those who idealize him and remove him from our humanity). But the startling truth that comes to us now from the Jesus we see in Gethsemane is that because he experienced weakness, suffering, and temptation, he is able to sympathize with us.

The second lesson that comes to us from this garden episode attests to *the veracity of the evangelists*. It is extraordinary that this story was so faithfully preserved by the Gospel writers. Let me remind you that the Gospels are not historical biographies in the modern sense. Rather, it is their purpose to bear witness to Jesus in order to elicit faith in him. For this reason, the writers were selective in their material, and it would be natural for them to include stories which magnify Jesus and omit those which present him in a poor light.

Yet, here Jesus is in Gethsemane recoiling in horror from death; sorrowing, weeping, sweating, and praying that if possible the cup may pass from him. Unfriendly critics of Christianity would be sure to use this story to discredit Jesus and to claim that many martyrs have gone to their death more bravely than he did. So the fact that the Synoptic writers incorporate the story, in-

15

cluding both the horror of Jesus in prospect of his death and the reprehensible sleepiness of his apostles, is one of many phenomena in the Gospels which confirms our confidence in their reliability.

So why was it included? The three writers seem to lay their emphasis on the contrast between the prayer of Jesus and the prayerlessness of the apostles. Three times Jesus asked them to watch with him while he went away to pray, and three times he came back to find them asleep. The Gospel writers seem to be saying that the agony of Jesus is an experience we cannot share, whereas the sleep of the apostles is an example we must not copy, at least if we value our Christian stability.

The agony of Jesus

In recording the Gethsemane story, Matthew and Mark say that Jesus was "greatly disturbed and troubled," using words which denote both amazement and alarm. He himself said, "My soul is very sorrowful, even to death." Because of the greatness of his burden, he took Peter, James, and John further into the garden with him. Then, going on alone he prostrated himself on the ground and prayed out loud with cries and tears, repeating his petitions. And it is Luke who adds a reference to the "agony" he experienced under tremendous strain which resulted in his bloody sweat.

Here was a crisis so intense that its symptoms were not merely emotional but also physical. What did it all mean? There is certainly no doubt that the reference is to his coming death. But why did he recoil from it when so many martyrs have met death with composure and even gaiety? Was Jesus afraid of the scourging and crucifixion? Was he a coward in the hour of his testing? Absolutely not! Such an interpretation must be rejected completely because all the evidence of his former life contradicts it and so does his later demeanor when eventually he comes to suffer and die.

But what Jesus was really shrinking from was something far worse than physical torture by crucifixion. He referred to it as "this cup." He pictured a cup being offered him by the Father, and shrank from drinking it. The Old Testament imagery tells us what this meant: A cup in the hand of God was a recognized symbol of his judgment, of his righteous wrath against sin. For example, in Isaiah 51:17 we read, "Rouse yourself, stand up O Jerusalem, you who have drunk at the hand of the Lord the cup of his wrath."

What Jesus shrank from was not death as an experience of pain, but death as the penalty for sin; not physical death at the hands of the Romans, but spiritual death at the hand of his Father; not the nails which would tear his flesh, but the sins which he would bear upon his soul. It wasn't the moment when all his disciples would forsake him, but a far worse experience of being forsaken which would force from his lips that awful cry, "My God, my God, why have you forsaken me?" Jesus knew that he was to endure the wrath or judgment of God—the God-forsakenness which we deserve because of our sin and guilt. No wonder he cried out to be spared from it! It is a prayer we can never echo. Suffering and pain we have to bear, but not the anguish of sin-bearing or the pains of hell. Only Jesus, the spotless God-man, could do that.

17

The Gift of Easter

The sleep of the apostles

During those moments in the garden both Jesus and his apostles were on the threshold of testing. Although his own ordeal was unique, yet both he and they were to face fanatical opposition. Both knew they would be tempted to compromise. How did they prepare? Jesus prayed, but the apostles slept.

Jesus prayed not only that the cup should pass from him but that God's will might be done. Luke tells us that an angel appeared to strengthen him. One thing we know for sure: He emerged from his agony with complete serenity. When Peter drew his sword and tried to protect him, Jesus said, "Shall I not drink the cup which my Father has given me?" And later before his judges when he was accused, insulted, and mocked, we are astonished by his unflinching courage and unruffled calm.

But what happened to the apostles in their moments of crisis? "They all forsook him and fled." Three times Peter totally disowned him, even with curses and oaths.

Why this ignominious behavior? They were completely unprepared. Jesus had urged them to "watch and pray that you may not enter into [succumb to] temptation." Now, we certainly can feel sympathetic with the apostles. Sleep is a natural demand of the human body, and they were desperately tired. Nevertheless, Jesus knew they would never stand against temptation if they didn't pray, and for this reason he kept waking them up. "The spirit is willing, but the flesh is weak," he said. That is, we have a desire to pray (it is a sign that we are Christians), but we are frail and fallen humans and our performance doesn't match our desire.

Watch and Pray

Twice the apostles thought they could meet the emergency with force. When Jesus spoke of his coming death, they said, "Look Lord, here are two swords" (Luke 22:38). And when Judas arrived at the garden with his detachment of officials to arrest Jesus, they asked, "Lord, shall we strike with the sword?" (Luke 22:49). But Jesus' kingdom is not of this world, so he responded, "Put up your sword." As Earl Ellis comments, "Eager to fight God's war with man's weapons . . . , the disciples fumble with the weapon that counts." And we, too, must remember that our warfare is spiritual—not of the world—and the weapons of our warfare must be spiritual also; prayer is the chief among them.

Here, then, is the vivid contrast, word-painted so effectively by the Gospel writers. Where did Jesus get his incredible calm and courage? Answer: he prayed! Why did the apostles fail him so abysmally? Answer: they slept!

It is utterly impossible, it seems to me, to reflect on this Gethsemane scene without confronting certain extremely piercing questions.

By any chance, are you a lonely Christian in a non-Christian environment, tempted to deny Christ or run away?

Are you beset by some fierce temptation—to jealousy, malice, lust, temper, pride?

Are you single when you long to be married? Or if you are married, is your marriage threatened and crippled by strain?

A yes answer to any or all of these provokes further questions: Do you sleep when you ought to be praying? Your spirit is willing . . . but is your flesh weak? Most certainly, we all must learn to discipline our

19

flesh. The prophet says that only those who "wait on the Lord" renew their strength (Isa. 40:31), and Jesus commands us to "watch and pray."

So then, if we marvel at the serenity of Jesus and the faithlessness of the apostles in this acute moment of crisis, let us always remember that they slept while he prayed.

I Am the Resurrection
and the Life

Richard C. Halverson

". . . I am the resurrection and the life; he who believes in me, though he die, yet shall he live, and whoever lives and believes in me shall never die" (John 11:25-26).

THE MOST COMPELLING ARGUMENT for the supreme relevance of Jesus Christ as the only adequate Savior in history is found in his words at the grave of Lazarus. Here, without question is the most astounding "I am" claim which Jesus ever made.

From the human perspective we have one, inevitable, universal problem or enemy—death. It is the ultimate frustration in all of life and history. Throughout all of time death has aborted the best laid plans and finest dreams of people. From the small and intimate family circle to the complexities of national and international intrigue, death has laid waste some of mankind's dearest hopes. And we can only speculate about how often a medical or scientific breakthrough which has vast lifesaving potential is delayed because of the death of a researcher who is on the brink of discovery.

Is there a solution to this universal problem? Can this dreaded enemy which strikes terror into the hearts of people everywhere be defeated? Good questions!

It is interesting to recall that history is loaded with accounts of saviors—messiahs—who have made extravagant claims, who have espoused cure-all answers to life's greatest dilemmas. In fact, Arnold Toynbee in his monumental work, *The Study of History*, devotes one entire chapter to the subject of saviors. He breaks them down into four categories: the savior with a scepter—the political savior; the savior with the book—the philosopher, teacher, theologian; the savior with the sword—the military type; and the man-god or god-man saviors—those of Greek and Norse mythology. Professor Toynbee points out then that each of these savior types ultimately capitulates to the great enemy, death. Politicians, kings, military leaders, philosophers, all die. And each of the demi-gods of history has likewise succumbed to the same enemy. Then he concludes this significant chapter with these words, "When the last civilization shall have come to the river of death, there on the other side filling the whole horizon with Himself will be *the Savior.*" In the mind of this great historian there is only one Savior who is qualified to save—because he conquered death.

What an absolutely incredible claim Jesus made when he said, "I am the resurrection and the life; he who believes in me, though he die, yet shall he live, and whoever lives and believes in me shall never die."

Let's examine the middle claim of Jesus first: ". . . he who believes in me, though he die, yet shall he live . . ." This compelling statement was made two thousand years ago—Jesus laid down his life on Calvary's cross and then conquered death three days later on that first Easter—these events occurred at a precise moment in history. But the testimony of Christ and the Bible goes beyond that. The death and resurrection of Jesus are equally relevant for *all* of history—past, present, and future.

To illustrate: In another of Jesus' amazing "I am" claims, he said, "Before Abraham was, I am." Now, this statement certainly mystified the people who heard it. After all, Abraham had lived two thousand years before. Yet, somehow, Abraham had anticipated the death and ressurection of Jesus; his hope lay in Christ.

Then there is the startling account of the appearance of Moses and Elijah with Jesus on the occasion of his transfiguration. Even though Moses and Elijah had lived hundreds of years before, there they stood that day—alive, visible—talking with Jesus. And according to the Scripture, Peter and James and John recognized them.

The eleventh chapter of Hebrews illuminates an amazing panorama of faith. Beginning with Abel and continuing on through the prophets, the writer offers forceful thumbnail sketches of heroic faith. But the key to even a partial comprehension of their faith in view of the times in which they lived is to realize that the hope of these who predated the time of Jesus by hundreds and even thousands of years was, in fact, fulfilled in the resurrection of Christ.

The astounding fact of the Christian faith, and one that is so difficult to accept and understand, is that the hope we have in Jesus Christ is not only for the present and the future, but it is retroactive for all of the past, even from the beginning of time. It is precisely at this point that all of the fantasized utopias of mankind fall short. Even if they were to materialize, their benefit would be felt only by those who were alive at that time and in the future.

This is indeed the futility at the very heart of history. Every system, including democracy and capitalism, is inadequate in that no hope is offered for an Abraham, a Noah, or a Moses. But the hope which Christ offers blankets all of time: ". . . though he were dead, yet shall he live . . ." Here is the promise of a future for all who have died in the past—life eternal.

Then Jesus unleashed these startling words, ". . . whoever lives and believes in me shall never die."

I Am the Resurrection and the Life

The importance of what is really meant here cannot be exaggerated. It is a promise we tend to forget so easily—at least our behavior testifies frequently to our inconsistency. So often as a pastor I have been amazed at the blatant display of raw paganism at the funeral of one who was a Christian. Far too much is made over the body which is being laid away. However it is handled, in time it will return to the dust from which it came. But that is not important, for at the proper moment in the future that Christian loved one or friend will be resurrected in a new, incorruptible, and immortal body.

Similarly, I believe that much of our grief is un-Christian. Don't misunderstand me, though. There is a sharp distinction between grieving because of our personal loss and in grieving for that loved one because he or she has been "robbed of a future." So often we've heard it said, "How sad. He had so much to live for; he had such a bright future."

It is pagan to treat the death of a Christian loved one as if it were a loss for him or her. Paul affirmed that "to die is gain." As a matter of fact, the word for death in the Bible signifies a move, a liberation. It is the same word as "exodus." It means emancipation from the slavery of a physical body that is really not adequate for human aspirations. At that moment which we call death, the personality, the person, who inhabited that body is liberated. *Loved ones who have died in Christ have never been more alive.*

But of supreme importance and significance is the emphasis and the order of Jesus' words to Mary and Martha when he said, "*I* am the resurrection and the life." Yes, they and we tend to view this reference only as to a future event—a specific time when the Son of

27

God returns to this earth, graves are opened, and new, immortal, and incorruptible bodies rise from the dust and ashes. And at that same time everyone who is alive and believes in Jesus will be changed—their mortal shells being replaced with immortal and incorruptible bodies.

The reference in this particular phrase of Scripture, however, is to far more than an event; it is to a Person— to an "I." John said, "In him was life." And here Jesus said, "I am . . . life." If we believe in Jesus Christ, he lives in us—now! Actually, if we understand our Bible correctly, it teaches that the person who believes in Christ is alive because *the only life he has is in Christ.* Remember the words of Paul: "I have been crucified with Christ; it is no longer I who live, but Christ who lives in me; and the life I now live in the flesh I live by faith in the Son of God, who loved me and gave himself for me" (Gal. 2:20).

Christ in me—that is eternal, resurrection life. As Christians, *we are eternally alive!* And because resurrection life resides in a Person, our basic need is a relationship with that Person. It is not believing a lot of things *about* him, but believing *in* him, accepting what he said and did.

Then follows the penetrating question to Mary and Martha, and that same question has reverberated down through all of history: "Do you believe this?" Belief— the profoundest issue to confront the human race.

The first belief-confrontation occurred in the Garden of Eden when God said, "You may freely eat of every tree of the garden; but of the tree of the knowledge of good and evil you shall not eat, for in the day that you eat of it you shall die" (Gen. 2:16–17). But when the serpent appeared on the scene, he contradicted God and asserted, "You will not die." Now, Eve had to make a choice: believe God or the serpent. And it was her tragic decision to place belief in the serpent that repudiated her own perfection and that of the entire human race. Now, however, according to Jesus' words, that perfection can be restored—in him. Restoration was the purpose for his entering human history almost two thousand years ago, and in God's time he will return to consummate that restoration.

It is extremely important that we recognize the subtlety of that original temptation in the garden. The serpent was actually saying to Eve, "Don't believe in God; believe in yourself." This is humanism . . . have faith in yourself . . . believe in human institutions and systems. But belief in yourself or in human institutions is the very antithesis of our Christian faith, wherein our confidence and total trust is in Jesus Christ. However, Satan introduced the deadly "belief in yourself" concept in the Garden of Eden, and it has infected the entire human race in all subsequent generations.

Our Bible unfolds a tragic record of human failure from the time of Adam and Eve's original perfection in the garden right down to the present moment. But there is something within each of us that does not want to believe in the bumbling failure of the human effort. We want to put our trust and faith in a person. That is why we're constantly looking for a politician or a philosopher or a great military leader to emerge with ready-made solutions for our human dilemmas. And this may well happen out ahead when the anti-christ ushers in what will be "the worst of times."

Believe in God or believe in man? This is the fundamental issue that confronts every person. It was true in Eden; it was the ultimate question at the tomb of Lazarus; and it is the underlying issue in these twilight years of the twentieth century.

We are not, however, left without help in confronting and responding to this question. The good news of the gospel for the past, present, and future came through loud and clear at the grave of Lazarus when Jesus enunciated the one solution for human failure— the one alternative to death: "I am the resurrection and the life; he who believes in me, though he die, yet shall he live, and whoever lives and believes in me shall never die."

*The Resurrection and
Future Identity*

D. Elton Trueblood

For I delivered to you as of first importance what I also received, that Christ died for our sins in accordance with the scriptures, that he was buried, that he was raised on the third day in accordance with the scriptures (1 Cor. 15:3-4).

It Is Most Unfortunate that in normal experience we face the fact of the resurrection only once a year. Of course, that is better than not facing it at all. But it is important for us to realize that in following this practice we have abandoned the pattern set for us by the early Christians. For with them, the resurrection theme was both a constant and central emphasis.

You will recall how the Apostle Paul outraged the Athenians and especially the Epicurean and Stoic philosophers by including a mention of the resurrection in his famous address on Mars Hill. And again in the first letter to the Corinthians Paul reminded them of the terms under which he preached the gospel: "For I delivered to you as of first importance what I also received, that Christ died for our sins in accordance with the scriptures, that he was buried, that he was raised on the third day in accordance with the scriptures, and that he appeared to Cephas, then to the twelve. Then he appeared to more than five hundred brethren at one time, most of whom are still alive, though some have fallen asleep. Then he appeared to James, then to all the apostles. Last of all, as to one untimely born, he appeared to me. Whether then it was I or they, so we preach and so you believed" (1 Cor. 15:3–8, 11).

If we face the history of the gospel realistically, we are forced to the conclusion that apart from the belief in the resurrection of Christ there would never have been an enduring church. Following the trial of Jesus and his death on the cross, the apostles were beaten, cowardly, discouraged, and disappointed men. They had returned to their homes and former tasks believing that the cause in which they had been recruited had ended in abject failure. But just a few days later their whole mood was changed to one of victory and hope. And the only explanation we have for this amazing reversal is that Christ had actually risen from the dead and they had encountered him in person. They were convinced that he was alive, and it was this conviction which made the church possible.

It is vitally important for us today to understand what the resurrection means as applied to ordinary persons like ourselves and our loved ones. It is indeed significant that both The Apostles' Creed and The Nicene Creed end with statements concerning the resurrection. The conclusion of The Apostles' Creed involves two phrases: "The resurrection of the body; and the life everlasting." And the final sentence of The Nicene Creed is: "And we look for the resurrection of the dead and the life of the world to come."

The point most difficult for modern men and women is that of the resurrection of the body. Even though thousands upon thousands of people repeat these phrases every Sunday, I suspect that many write them off in their own minds as antique and meaningless espressions. Since they know that our physical bodies decay, belief in the resurrection of the body seems incredible. Nevertheless, as we study the term more carefully, we begin to realize that it stands for something exceedingly meaningful.

I believe the heart of the meaning of the resurrection of the body is found in the conviction that the recognition of individuals will be part of the world to come. The body, whether physical or spiritual, is our means of recognition. The classic passage on this belief is found in 1 Corinthians 15. It is stressed here that the resurrected body will not be the physical one we now know, but it will be something entirely different: a spiritual body. Here indeed is a vivid affirmation of the fact that God can and will give us other means of recognizing each other after the disintegration of our physical bodies.

The very heart of the Christian faith rests on the notion that individuals are what count. If we were to have mere immortality, in the sense that each spirit is reunited with a general spirit, thus losing its identity like a drop of water when it flows back into the ocean, this would not represent the saving of what is most precious to us. Furthermore, according to the teachings of Jesus Christ, it would not represent a saving of what is most precious in God's estimation. Jesus taught that God counts each of us as important and valuable and worth saving. And Christ's defense in his teaching of his faith in the life everlasting was his conviction of the unending and undefeatable care of the Father for each one.

We know a great deal about Christianity when we come to realize that Easter Day is not a celebration of immortality in some vague, philosophical sense of the word. Rather, it is a triumphant, glad, and victorious affirmation of the resurrection in the sense that individuality is preserved and glorified.

How is this possible? That is a valid question because we know that our means of recognizing one another in these present bodies is determined by such physical characteristics as the shape of our nose, the coloration of our hair, the contours of the face and head and body. But it is hard for us to imagine a non-physical means of recognition. The only answer we can come up with to this problem is to recognize our own ignorance. But let's look at it this way: If a dog or a cat were lounging in a room where we were holding an animated conversation, it would hear sounds but in most instances it would have no idea of what was being said or of the meaning. In like manner we may be as much beneath the level in which spiritual bodies make sense as the dog or cat is beneath the human level of understanding. There must be so much in the world around us which is real, but of which we in our finitude are not aware.

If anyone believes that the resurrection of the body is irrational simply because we cannot visualize it, I would say that denial of the resurrection of Jesus Christ is even more irrational. This was expressed in an unforgettable way by Professor George Herbert Palmer, a member of the brilliant galaxy of philosophers at Harvard some fifty years ago, on the occasion of the death of his wife, Alice Freeman Palmer, the president of Wellesley College. Speaking of her death, he said, "Who can contemplate the fact of it and not call the universe irrational if, out of deference to a few particles of disordered material, it should exclude so fair a spirit?"

This is the point precisely. The life of the world to come is indeed a mystery, but everything that we really know is also a mystery. The late Professor Whitehead of Harvard made this point so insistently that his students could not miss it. He pointed out so beautifully that even as we cannot know how personality *can survive,* there is no way we can know how personality *has arrived.* How strange it is that out of a

The Gift of Easter

world of matter—of stars, of earth, of sand—there should arise beings who are able to think, to love, to know one another, to criticize themselves, and even to love God. *But we know that this has occurred.* For this reason, the future which we are unable to comprehend is no more mysterious than the present which we *do* know. There is a sense, then, in which the final word of wisdom on this most important of subjects is, "Brethren, we are the sons of God and it doth not yet appear what we shall be."

What Difference Does it Make?

Ray C. Stedman

If Christ has not been raised, then our preaching is in vain.
. . . If Christ has not been raised your faith is futile and you
are still in your sins. Then those also who have fallen asleep
in Christ have perished. If for this life only we have hoped in
Christ, we are of all men most to be pitied. But in fact
Christ has been raised from the dead. . . . For as by a man
came death, by a man has come also the resurrection of the
dead. For as in Adam all die, so also in Christ shall all be
made alive (1 Cor. 15:14,17-22).

WHAT IF JESUS CHRIST did not emerge from the garden tomb on that first Easter morning? What if it didn't happen? Would it make a difference?

Certainly, we are not the first to ponder these questions. The Apostle Paul and others among the first century Christians wrestled with them. In effect, many early believers said, "We can't be sure. The idea that a person could actually rise from the dead—break the bonds of death by himself—and come back again is an almost unbelievable claim." And it is.

Yet, in 1 Corinthians 15 Paul argued these questions and came up with some startling and shocking conclusions.

First, he said that if Jesus did not rise from the dead, then for all practical purposes, Christianity is a waste of time. Imagine! Even though Christianity presents some very brave and lofty ideas in rather exotic language at times, except for the resurrection of Jesus, it is just the wishful thinking of people who are tired of coping with life's heartaches and want something beautiful to cling to. And if this were true, the New Testament is nothing more than the story of a deluded dreamer who claimed powers he didn't have and who kidded himself and others into believing he was somebody he really wasn't.

Now, let's carry our thinking on this a bit further. If this is the case, then all of the wonderful writings in the New Testament must be thrown aside as worthless. And among others, this would have to include the noble statements Jesus uttered in the Sermon on the Mount. Let's face it, the concepts Jesus talked about there are certainly contrary to the way we naturally think. They exalt and highly value principles which most people believe are unworkable. For example, when Jesus said, "Blessed are the poor in spirit"—the bankrupt people who have come to the end of themselves and realize they don't have what it takes to handle life—he certainly was going contrary to the ideas shared by most people of his time and ours. The world is basically committed to the policy, "Blessed are the pushers, the aggressive people, the self-confident, the ones who know what they're doing." But this is just the opposite of what Jesus said. And if he didn't rise from the dead, those words aren't worth the paper they are written on. The same is true of Paul's concluding words in 1 Corinthians 13, "Now abide faith, hope and love, these three; but the greatest of these is love." Except for the fact of the resurrection, these words are sentimental nonsense.

If Jesus didn't rise from the dead, we would really have to write off the entire New Testament. You just can't say "I'll accept this but not that part," because it all hangs on the fact that Jesus was who he said he was and could do what he said he could. And if he didn't rise from the dead, that just isn't true.

The same can also be said for the Old Testament. Its predictions all looked forward to the One who was to come—the One who would achieve what man had never been able to realize. All its rituals point to a greater sacrifice, to Someone who would come to *be* the real sacrifice. Again, all the dreams and hopes and longings expressed in the poetic language of the prophet Isaiah and others, pointing to a golden age, are reduced to dusty and meaningless archaic stories unless the triumph of Easter is reality.

It is sobering to realize, too, that if Jesus didn't rise from the dead, we have no hope beyond this present life . . . the grave is the end. Many people believe that today. This pessimism is expressed in the eloquent but dreary words of Bertrand Russell, "The life of a man is a long march through the night, surrounded by invisible foes, tortured by weariness and pain, toward a goal which few can hope to reach and where none may tarry long. One by one as they march, our comrades vanish from our sight, seized by the silent orders of omnipotent death. Brief and powerless is man's life. On him and all his race the slow, sure doom falls pitiless and dark. Blind to good and evil, reckless of destruction, omnipotent matter rolls on its relentless way. For man, condemned today to lose his dearest, tomorrow himself to pass through the gate of darkness, it remains only to cherish, ere yet the blow falls, the lofty thoughts that ennoble his little day."

This note of hopelessness is echoed as well by the words of a popular song which expresses the idea that we're orphans in this world because there is no tomorrow. And if there is no tomorrow, we are, as Paul says, ". . . of all men most miserable."

If Jesus did not rise from the dead, we have no release from guilt and fear. We are locked into our sinful humanity and there is no way out. Forgiveness of sin is a meaningless expression. No power can deliver us from the fatal tendency within each of us to do what we don't want to do, and to fail again and again to achieve what we want to accomplish.

In fact, if the resurrection didn't happen, this whole business of Christianity is a joke, a big fraud, and we ought to forget it and struggle for the top of heap in the best way we can.

But let's turn our thinking now in another direction. What if Jesus Christ did rise from the dead as the Bible—our authority says? What difference does that mean to our late twentieth century world and to you and me?

The first and most obvious fact is that Jesus is still alive. He is with us. Imagine! This vigorous and rugged man who thoroughly captivated the people of his day by his life and ministry is still around; he is still available. The power and the compassion which characterized his life and which he promised to all who follow him is still loose in the world because he is alive and is available now to us. He can and does meet us now in the same way as when he was visibly walking the Palestinian roads.

If Jesus rose from the dead, that act validated his promises for all time. It poured life into these words, "Come unto me all who are weary and heavy laden and I will give you rest" . . . "He who follows me shall not walk in darkness but shall have the light of life" . . . "I am the door; if anyone enters by me, he will be saved, and will go in and out and find pasture" . . . "Peace I leave with you; my peace I give to you. Let not your hearts be troubled, neither let them be afraid" . . . "Be of good cheer, I have overcome the world."

The resurrection of Jesus also means that freedom from guilt and power to conquer our failures and weaknesses is still available to people. And this has been the Good News of the gospel for twenty centuries—that in coming to Jesus Christ, men and women find ability to rise above the locked-in evil within us. To be sure, none of us has arrived and offer a perfect pattern for accomplishing this except Jesus. But the moment the decision is made to follow Christ, the healing process begins, changes occur, and life is different.

Several years ago Tom Skinner, a noted black evangelist, charged twelve thousand young men and women at an Urbana Conference to "proclaim liberty to the captives. Give sight to the blind. Set at liberty them that are bruised. Go out to all the world and tell men who are bound mentally, spiritually, and physically that 'The Liberator has come!' " That is what the resurrection of Jesus means. The grave is not the end of the road; death does not have the last word. As Paul put it, "To depart and to be with Christ is far better." That amazing statement isn't just a faint and glimmering hope for Christians; it isn't a spiritual cliché to be repeated glibly when death approaches in order to steady us so we'll die well. No, indeed, it is a robust, positive certainty in thousands upon thousands of Christians' hearts as they come to the end of life. As a matter of fact, I heard recently of a Christian man who was told by his doctor that he was about to die and it made him so happy that, by the doctor's own testimony, the joy of the Spirit kept him alive for two more weeks. Because of the resurrection of Jesus we claim the eternal truth of the validity of *all* his promises, including those great words of hope, "Because I live, you shall live also . . ."

Then, of course, if Jesus rose from the dead, it means that the value of your life and mine will be determined by our relationship to that resurrection. In the Book of Acts we read about Paul's visit to Athens—that great center of education and culture and the city of Pericles,

Socrates, Plato, and Aristotle. In the midst of all the monuments to beauty and art and truth, which can still be seen in Athens, the Apostle insisted that all of this represented nothing more than the vain struggles of men to discover truth in the midst of life. Their search was ineffectual; nothing of their deepest problems had been solved. Standing on the slopes of Mars Hill, with the glory and beauty of the Acropolis in full view across the valley, Paul said, "The times of ignorance God overlooked, but now he commands all men everywhere to repent, because he has fixed a day on which he will judge the world in righteousness by a man whom he has appointed, and of this he has given assurance to all men by raising him [Jesus] from the dead" (Acts 17:30–31).

These words provoked consternation then, and they still do today. Nevertheless, the word is given here that ultimately we will all stand before the living and risen Lord Jesus. He is the Lord of the world. This is his universe and we must live by his rules. Ultimately our life will be judged and examined on his terms. If we link our lives with the world and its ways, if we live for its pleasures and its praise and its values, we will find ourselves joined to what the cross of Christ brought to a jolting halt. As someone has said, "Hell is nothing less than truth known too late." The Apostle John worded it this way, "If anyone loves the world, the love of the Father is not in him."

On the other hand, if we begin to live in the power of Jesus' resurrection, we will learn to live in the world—not withdrawn or isolated—in victory, drawing every day upon his forgiveness to recover from our failures and to be accepted in his presence. In resurrection life we can draw daily on his strength, his love, and his resources so we are able to meet the demands which life throws at us. And we can draw on the engulfing grace of our risen Lord who knows and understands us, has made ample provision for our weakness and failure, and who picks us up again and again and carries us through—not away from life's situations and dilemmas but right through the midst of them.

It is from this vantage point in life we discover that "the world passes away and the lusts thereof; but he who does the will of God abides forever."

Having examined the proof and the promises of the resurrection, we can now say with total confidence that there is no joy like a Christian's joy . . . no peace like the peace of God . . . no love like the love of Christ, which forgives and heals and restores. Savonarola of Florence, hundreds of years ago, expressed it this way, "They may kill me, but they can never, never, never tear the living Christ out of my heart."

Here is the message of the power of the resurrection. None of us today live perfectly. We're in all stages of the process of healing. In fact, the church is a sort of clinic where people are being healed. There aren't perfect people among us, but we've found One who has the answer and he's working it out hour by hour, day by day.

God *has* fulfilled his word in the resurrection of Jesus Christ, and it does make a difference. His promises are eternally true. Among the closing words of our Bible we read, "Behold, I stand at the door and knock; if anyone hears my voice and opens the door, I will come in to him . . ." (Rev. 3:20). "I will come in to him . . ." what an astounding promise, but it's true and it is ours. Jesus lives, and so do we!

The Easter Perspective

John R. Claypool

Therefore, since we are surrounded by so great a cloud of witnesses, let us also lay aside every weight, and sin which clings so closely, and let us run with perseverance the race that is set before us, looking to Jesus the pioneer and perfecter of our faith, who for the joy that was set before him endured the cross, despising the shame, and is seated at the right hand of God (Heb. 12:1-2).

SOME TIME AGO, GORDON COSBY of the Church of the Saviour in Washington, D.C., was asked to speak to the children of his congregation on what the Bible teaches us about life. He was urged to make this as practical and down-to-earth as possible.

What he came up with was astonishingly simple and concrete: First, that the Bible pictures life as getting better and better as it goes along; that is, it is better to be a child than an infant, better to be an adolescent than a child, better to be an adult than an adolescent, and it is better to be aged than just an adult. Second, life gets harder and harder as it goes along; that is, it is harder to be a child than an infant, harder to be an adolescent than a child, harder to be an adult than an adolescent, harder to be aged than just an adult.

Now, these assertions weren't exactly what we might have expected. In fact, they seem sparse, plain, and rather inelegant. However, the important question is: Are they true? What are we to make of this paradoxical combination of images as a way of describing our journey through history? Does life get better and better and harder and harder as it goes along?

Probably, our initial reaction to this assertion is ambiguous. One part of the formula is obviously true. Who can deny that life gets harder and harder as it goes along? All we have to do is compare the agony of adolescence with childhood, or the ambiguities of adulthood with adolescence, or the pain of old age and retirement to earlier adulthood, to realize that the challenges of life do escalate the further we go. This is a fact that artists of all times have recognized. For example, Eugene O'Neill entitled the play which was in fact his autobiography *Long Day's Journey into Night*. The image here is that light is gradually giving way to darkness as it moves along. If one were diagramming it by means of color, the brightest part would be the beginning, then the progression would be to the more subdued tones, until at last comes nothing but unrelieved darkness into which everything flows.

It seems that from every direction the truth of one part of Cosby's formula is confirmed, and that calls the other part into question. It is the fact that life does get harder and harder as we go along which makes us doubt that it gets better and better. Gordon Cosby's words may sound more like a contradiction to us than a paradox. This is hardly the way we would look at life if left on our own.

But, having admitted that, I must go on to say that I believe this is a correct interpretation of the biblical witness. No matter how diametrically it cuts across our present feelings, this is the way the Bible pictures life—probably the reason it is called "a revelation." This is a word never used to describe something one already feels or believes. A revelation shocks and surprises—it isn't something we come up with on our own, and this is precisely the nature of the biblical way of looking at life.

You see, at bottom, biblical religion is a religion of promise, not one of nostalgia. From its earliest beginnings, its thrust was toward the future. It was a religion of beckoning, of being drawn out toward what lay ahead. When God made contact with man, it was never from behind, but always from out ahead, out in the future—promising, beckoning. This is how God first approached Abraham and Moses and all the heroes of the faith. This explains why an Israelite always positioned his God differently from people of other religions. In response to the question, "Where is your God?" an Israelite never said, "Back there" or "In here" or even "Up there." Rather, he would say, "Out there"—pointing straight into the future. For he was the God of promise—to be found much more in what was coming than in what was going. He was always on the move toward "The Great Not Yet," and he invited Israel to go with him.

There was always a land of promise out ahead for Israel's God, and this, of course, is where the idea began that life gets better and better as it goes along. God was the power of the future, and as such, he could be depended upon to provide the resources which would be needed out ahead. This is also where the element of challenge comes in, for moving forward into the unknown is a difficult and demanding experience. After all, Abraham did have to leave his kinspeople and his familiar surrounding, and Moses ran into all kinds of hardships as he ventured forth on the promise. Life did get better and better in terms of greater fulfillment, but it also got harder and harder. However, the one proved to be the resource for the other. It was the experience of these men that formed the foundation of biblical religion. Here is when the paradox was born that life gets better and better and harder and harder as it goes along.

However, the perspective that began with Abraham did not come to completion until the advent of Jesus of Nazareth and the climactic event of Easter. Up until then, it was earthbound, limited to time and space, and this was a problem. How could life really get better and better if ultimately it ended in nothingness? How could the stage beyond agedness be called "better" and another challenge if it marked the cessation of all life?

To that final "boundary situation"—the experience of death—the resurrection of Jesus speaks, and without Easter the whole perspective would collapse. It needs to be realized that in the profoundest sense Jesus was the embodiment of the religion of promise. Better than anyone else, he assumed a forward-looking stance toward life. For him there was always a promised land out ahead, and life was a pilgrimage that ascended, rather than descended, that was challenging, but infinitely worth it. This attitude toward life became evident very early when, mother-like, Mary tried to hold Jesus back from the turbulence of adolescence and adulthood and keep him in dependence. For it was at this time he said in effect, "I cannot remain a child. I must be about my Father's business. I must go forward."

The first words of Jesus' public ministry reverberated with a promise, "The time is fulfilled. The kingdom of heaven is at hand. Repent and believe the gospel." This was a way of saying, "Something better than we have ever known is on the way, just ahead. Therefore, let us move from here and now, expectantly and hopefully, toward what is being given." And this was the keynote of his whole ministry. He always looked on what was coming as more promising than what was going, even though the difficulties increased. Toward the end he saw his opposition solidifying and the prospect of suffering taking shape, but even this did not divert him into a nostalgic retreat. Simon Peter attempted to turn Jesus around at Caesarea Philippi, implying that the suffering which lay ahead was not worth it, but Jesus labeled such talk the work of Satan—an effort to undo what God was trying to do. Instead, he "set his face toward Jerusalem."

The early church understood the stance of Christ quite well and could identify with the words of Scripture, "For the joy set before him, he endured the cross, despised the shame, and is set down at the right hand of God the Father."

Here was life getting better and better and harder and harder at the same time. But the event of Easter was needed to round out this perspective. If it had not been for the victory over death, we could not really say, "Life gets better and better as it goes along." How could that be true if death is a catch-all that marks the end of every life? Only by the event of resurrection is the pilgrimage of life set in an eternal context, and only then does the promise of Israel really come true— and the last stages of life remain adventure instead of disaster. Life cannot be said to get better and better for three score and ten, only then to disintegrate into nothingness. That would be decline and fall—a "long day's journey into night."

But Jesus Christ did not remain in the grave. He arose—finer, brighter, and more creative than ever before, and in doing so, he established light on the other side of the darkness of death and the possibility of endless maturing in the promise of God. Yes, it is the Easter event that makes the formula work—without it the claim could not stand. In light of it, however, the parts do fit together and can have fantastic significance for the life we're called on to live every day. Let's face it, the Easter perspective doesn't pertain only to the future; it speaks directly to one of the deepest problems of life—how do you keep going? Where do you get the strength to get up every morning and face a world that is different from what it was yesterday and promises to keep on changing more and more? What is there to live for out ahead?

This is the issue on which the Easter perspective sheds light. We are coming to realize more and more the functional importance of hope. It is as necessary an ingredient for the survival of the human spirit as are food and air for the body. We are all familiar with the old cliché, "As long as there is life, there is hope." But it is even truer to say, "As long as there is hope, there is life."

An illustration of this truth is found in an experiment which was conducted in the Psychology Department at the University of North Carolina. They took two rats and put them in containers half full of water. The first container was sealed and the rat instinctively realized there was no hope of escape, so in less than three minutes he gave up and drowned. The other container was only partially sealed—a possibility of escape and survival was left open. That rat swam for thirty-six hours straight before dying of exhaustion.

It makes all the difference in the world in terms of coping and courage whether or not you believe there is some "land of promise" out ahead. As Viktor Frankl learned in a concentration camp, if a man has something to live for, this will inspire "copability"—he will have reason to find out how to live. And this is the great gift of Easter and the biblical religion—it gives one a basis for hope and puts one in touch with a strength and courage that would not be possible on any other terms.

Referring back to Gordon Cosby's statement again, it is important to realize that the sequence is significant. We need first of all to hear that life gets better and better so that out of that prospect we can cope with the fact that it also gets harder and harder. How does this work, practically speaking, as we move through the stages of life? In my judgment the crucial and descriptive words are *trust* and *flexibility*—and neither one is easy. For example, deep down we all have the uneasy feeling that God cannot really be trusted to provide for us—that we must create our own security. This is why it is hard to move into the unknown and count on him to meet us there in adequacy. Moses had this problem when he saw the burning bush out in the desert. When God instructed him to go back to Egypt, he had a thousand fears about what he would do if this or that happened. But God seemed to be saying, "Be not afraid, I will be with you. This is my expedition, remember. When I propose, I provide. As thy days, so will thy strength be. Don't worry, just follow." And when Moses did this, he wasn't disappointed.

In a sense this is what Jesus was talking about when he warned against all efforts to try to save one's life. He said that was the surest way to lose it, for no one can successfully secure himself against all danger. If he tries to, he will only fail. Only the Creator can do that. Therefore, anyone who would save his life must lose it "into God." That is, we must trust him to provide, but this is so hard to do. We have trouble believing that the God who gives us our lives can be counted on to sustain them.

At the same time it is certainly not easy to accept the new circumstances that confront us as we move through life and be flexible enough to look in them for joy. Most of us tend to become very rigid in our likes and dislikes and demand that joy be given to us in the forms we already know and understand. We are always measuring the future by the past, and saying to God, "Encore! I want more and more of just the same." But God never does anything the same way twice. His creativity is so great that all time and space cannot exhaust him.

So often, though, we rebel against this divine creativity and say, "If life can't be the way it was, I don't want it." This was the sin of Lot's wife—she refused to look forward to what was coming, but kept looking back to what was going. And with profound symbolic insight, the writer of Genesis said that she turned into a pillar of salt—she became a dead, inorganic thing.

How different was the pattern of our Lord. He always sensed that promise was resident in the new. Even toward the end, when the shadow of the cross was becoming more and more inevitable, he faced it honestly with his disciples and said, "Don't despair. This is the Father's will. There is a promised land out ahead even here. It is best for you that I be taken." I'm sure the disciples found this to be an absurd statement. How could life without Jesus be better than life with him? But in the profoundest sense it turned out to be right. They would never have known how much the Father loved them had it not been for the cross. And they would never have come to the maturity they achieved had he remained with them bodily, for they would have continued to depend totally on him.

Here was life being given on a different set of terms, and the challenge was: Could they be flexible enough to look for the blessing in the new rather than lament the passing of the old? This remains one of the central challenges of the Christian life—can I receive the gifts of each day and not make idols out of them? Can I learn to let certain treasures go when the time comes—gratefully and not bitterly—in the confidence that gifts of greater value are being given in the new? The first shape of something that is unknown is never as appealing as familiar joys, but it may be the best thing that has ever happened to us. This stance of acceptance and flexibility toward life has to be the greatest day-to-day challenge I know, but I am confident this is the way we were meant to see life and live it.

I can affirm that the formula is correct. Life does get better and better as it goes along, even though it gets harder and harder. This is the biblical perspective: There is promise out ahead, and the promise provides the strength to meet the challenge. So, lift up your hearts. Life is not "a long day's journey into night." St. Paul knew better: "Now we see through a glass darkly; but then face to face. Now I know in part, but then I shall know even as also I am known." Rather, life is a long night's journey into day, an inclining plane into unending becoming and maturing and joy.

How do we know? Because of Easter. Christ Jesus has risen from the dead. He who lived by the promise was not disappointed. His life did get harder and harder, to be sure. But it also got better and better! "Seeing then that we are encompassed about with this great cloud of witnesses, let us lay aside every weight that so easily besets us, and run with patience the race that is set before us, looking unto Jesus, the Author and Finisher of our faith, who, for the joy that was set before him, endured the cross, despised the shame, and sits at the right hand of God the Father."

The Last Fraud

David Poling

"Therefore order the sepulchre to be made secure until the third day, lest his disciples go and steal him away, and tell the people, 'He has risen from the dead,' and the last fraud will be worse than the first" (Matt. 27:64).

IN HIS VOLUME, *Grand Deception,* Alexander Klein has gathered the fascinating accounts of some of the major impostors, frauds, and hoaxes which have operated in world history. Through this research he has uncovered those amazing personalities who met kings, entertained presidents, inspected battleships, and attended international conferences under the pure disguise of false credentials.

Klein points out that there are at least three main categories into which we may identify those persons who become impersonators, carry forged documents, and pose as something they are not.

First, there is the profit motive. This covers all those schemes which people promote to make money off the gullibility of their victim. Yes, surprising as it may seem, people still try to sell the Brooklyn Bridge, still solicit sales for Florida real estate which turns out to be nothing more than a tired swamp. And promoters still offer shares of stock which represent, at best, a swindler's imagination. The hunger for quick gain pushes promoters into criminal designs and comprises the largest segment of those described in *Grand Deception.*

Then there are those people who like to be impersonators for the fun of it. I know a man in New York who appears regularly on radio talk shows either as an automotive expert or a witchcraft specialist and whose only background and expertise is his nerve and glibness of speech. He enjoys putting other people "on," and fulfills this role with style and assurance. He is happy and harmless. For him, April Fool's Day is a twelve month operation.

But the most tragic figures which Klein describes are those individuals who masquerade in the guise of the person they failed to become. There is the young student who fails to qualify for medical school and several years later slips into a small, midwestern town as the new "doctor"; the man who always dreamed of teaching in a college classroom and never had the funds to finish his own education, but five years later he is hired as Assistant Professor of History in a church college—complete with a bogus diploma and advanced degrees. Ultimately, he is exposed as a fraud and dismissed even though he was doing a good job otherwise.

So we conclude that there are frauds for money, frauds for the fun of it, and frauds who follow the road of deception out of a frustrated dream or a smashed career.

One of the most tragic figures in the field of deceptive art may well have been the Dutch painter, Hans Van Meegren. A student of seventeenth century master Vermeer, Hans made millions of dollars, according to some experts, by processing copies of the originals and selling them to an art starved public. For nearly four years he experimented with oils, solubles, and pigments. By baking his reproductions in an oven, he was able to deceive fine art dealers and their infra-red lamps. It is reported that he sold one work for $378,000.

But his fraud was finally discovered, and when he was brought to trial, he was asked why he was involved in such a deception. Hans blamed the critics! He said that his own creative work had been put down by the experts, and he burned under their judgment—that he was without talent or imagination. So he decided to show them—to teach them a lesson about their so-called competence, their arrogant understanding of painting. Thus, a mediocre painter became a master forger of rare art—all from the heartbreak of a meager following and a broken heart.

With this background on imposters, frauds, and hoaxes, it seems very strange and bewildering to read the words of our Scripture in Matthew 27:64 where the term "fraud" is fastened to the person of Jesus Christ. It is almost inconceivable from our vantage point that our Lord could have been accused of being a fraud, but he was.

In fact, the first charge brought by the accusers of Jesus was that he was an impostor because he claimed to be a king. On this charge, primarily, he was executed—although he said that his kingdom was not of this world. It is important for us to remember, though, that throughout his entire ministry his family, friends, and the masses that thronged after him were at times puzzled and confused by his role. And I believe that Jesus understood this because of his patient response to the followers of John the Baptist when they queried him as to whether he was *the one* or should they wait for another: "Go and tell John what you hear and see: the blind receive their sight and the lame walk, lepers are cleansed and the deaf hear, and the dead are raised up, and the poor have good news preached to them" (Matt. 11:4).

The life and teaching of Jesus was validated in the lives of those who followed him. It was also confirmed through his judgment of the times—upon their earthly kingdoms and the accommodations so cleverly constructed between imperial Rome and ecclesiastical Israel. You recall that at the beginning of Holy Week Jesus had pointed to the temple complex and predicted that it would be destroyed completely. For the religious establishment of that day this was sheer blasphemy, uttered by an impostor who pretended to deliver spiritual truths. It was unthinkable that the great temple would ever be destroyed or desecrated. Yet in a brief sixty years it was burned and leveled by the armies of Titus. Caesar himself had directed the final catastrophic campaign against fortified Jerusalem. The Romans attacked during Passover when hundreds of thousands of Jews flooded the holy city. Jewish historian Josephus records that on one day five hundred Jews were crucified in front of the gates of the beleaguered city. . . .

And Jerusalem fell,
And the temple fell,
And the nation was scattered,
With young men going to the mines
And women and children into slavery
And miserable others to the entertainment of the
   animals at Rome.

Yes, Jesus knew this people—their hopes and ambitions and secret promotions. "Seek first the kingdom of heaven," the "impostor" said, but they would not hear his words and now had to suffer his prophecy. He knew two kingdoms—one served by man and the other serving God. And during the centuries which have followed, we have come to know without question which one endures.

Then, too, Jesus was also charged with being a fraud. The authorities had heard it predicted that he would be raised from the dead. So they rushed to Pilate and asked for a double guard and a careful sealing of the tomb. All of this as a preventative against someone stealing the body as an embarrassment to the authorities—and "the last fraud will be worse than the first." As if the careful manipulations of mankind could frustrate the eternal purpose of God! And they didn't.

Was Jesus raised from the dead? The total experience of the first believers and of the latest followers is an affirmative answer to the question. It is my experience that the Christian life does not advance by theories; it is not sustained by classroom discussion or promoted by scholarly endorsements. Rather, the Christian life surges and grows when one comes to a faithful trust in God, in the reality of his Son—in belief in the resurrection of One who was known intimately by Peter and John and the others who had been with him before his death.

Brooks Atkinson, the distinguished drama critic of the *New York Times* for so many years—a person who has known thousands of actors and has seen hundreds of plays—said with the confidence that comes only from long experience that "all drama begins on Easter morning." Indeed, to omit the resurrection account in life and experience is to leave out the center of human existence and meaning.

But to each person, each seeker, this experience must be discovered afresh. When Albert Schweitzer pursued his study for his *The Quest for the Historical Jesus,* he sought to move beyond all the fragments of history and all the judgments of thousands of years of argument to find the real Jesus of the Gospels. Schweitzer concluded that one cannot trace the life of Christ through the imaginations and theories of others. Each one of us must experience our own encounter. And the meaning of resurrection faith, instead of being a fraud, comes clear as Schweitzer closed his work with these words:

> He comes to us as One unknown, without a name, as of old, by the lake-side, He came to those men who knew Him not. He speaks to us the same word: "Follow thou me!" and sets us to the tasks which he has to fulfil for our time. He commands. And to those who obey Him, whether they be wise or simple, He will reveal Himself in the toils, the conflicts, the sufferings which they shall pass through in His fellowship, and, as an ineffable mystery, they shall learn in their own experience Who He is (*The Quest for the Historical Jesus,* MacMillan, 1961).

The Christian is given the knowledge that the words of Jesus and the Spirit of Christ are not lost in this world . . . that the "Christ event" is not merely something that happened back someplace in sacred history . . . that to be a part of the Redeemed Fellowship is to know the truth which sets men free, now. Erich Fromm saw it in a proper light when he said, "The beginning of liberation lies in man's capacity to suffer." And the Christian takes not only his own share of suffering, but by the grace of God is able to reach out to his neighbor's pain and sorrow and anguish. Resurrection faith makes this an imperative.

Such was the pastoral work of Charles B. Smith, a minister in a Buffalo suburb. When an explosion and fire destroyed the music room of Cleveland Hill Junior High School in 1953, Mr. Smith visited the homes of the parents who lost children in the tragedy. The shock of the community, and the anguish of those who had to go out to find a casket for eleven- and twelve-year-old children was almost too much to bear. Fathers and mothers spoke of the comfort and caring and prayerful support that Mr. Smith gave as Christian and neighbor. He spoke to their condition out of the resources of his faith, and out of his understanding for their grief in a personal way, for one of the fourteen children lost in the school fire was his youngest daughter, Reba.

As we Christians are part of the world with its accidents, calamities, and disasters, we share the sorrow and heartache of all that happens, yet we are given something more—something that belongs to the people of God: the confidence that CHRIST IS RISEN, that "the last fraud" has become the champion of a living and lasting faith.

Encounters with Christ

Charles H. Huffman

It was late that Sunday evening, and the disciples were gathered together behind locked doors, because they were afraid of the Jews. Then Jesus came and stood among them. "Peace be with you," he said. And saying this, he showed them his hands and his side. The disciples were filled with joy at seeing the Lord (John 20:19-20, TEV).

HUDDLED TOGETHER BEHIND CLOSED and locked doors, paralyzed with fear—this is the description of Jesus' disciples just a few hours after that first Easter morning. Even though Mary Magdalene had told them earlier of her experience in the garden, it was incomprehensible. And they were fearful for their safety. After all, their leader had been executed and there was a good chance they would face similar charges. Also, there was a possibility now that they would be charged with body snatching, for in spite of the heavy stone and the Roman guard, the body of Jesus was missing.

It is easy to believe and understand the disciples' state of mind in this desperate situation. We can identify with that. But what is hard to believe is that without warning the crucified Jesus appeared and "stood among them." It was hard for them to believe what they saw—only after they examined his nail-pierced hands and wounded side were they filled with joy and their anxiety subsided.

But what is still harder for us to believe is the fact that Christ continues to encounter Christians today. Personal encounter with Jesus Christ did not stop when he moved beyond the vision of his disciples in that dramatic scene found in Acts 1:9. This is hard for us to accept because for so long we have worshiped the process of analytical argument and played down every other way to knowledge until we feel our intellectual integrity is insulted at the suggestion of such a revela-

74

tion. Then, too, we don't want to be disappointed or considered odd by others.

I'm inclined to believe, though, that the big reason we find it hard to believe is our fear of the consequences. It is intensely disturbing to open ourselves up and be vulnerable even to God himself if there is a chance that the convenient lifestyles we've fashioned, the priorities we've established to meet our needs, might be interrupted or altered. Rather than face such a radical possibility, we escape into the routine, and like Peter—"Go fishing." Or we have our car serviced or mow the lawn—go buy a suit or a dress. We'll do anything to avoid the responsibility of encounter.

But according to the New Testament story, Peter was confronted by the resurrected Christ at the shore while he was fishing. That's like meeting Christ at the supermarket or on the golf course. And that is just the point of John's entire Gospel. It is a record of spiritual encounters in the "now," in contemporary experience, in the routines of life.

However, for me the question this story raises is not did it happen in AD 29, but does it happen now? And from the standpoint of total honesty, we seem to be a bit ambivalent about believing that it does—we would like to believe, but we are afraid of the idea. We would like to believe that bolts and bars—cages we shut ourselves in for safety—are not the final condition for us, that in some way Christ would penetrate and say, "Peace be with you." We would like to believe the doctor's verdict is not the final word . . . that materialism is not life's final answer . . . that someone is in control of our destiny other than public opinion, economic advisors, scientists, politicians, and Arabian oil lords. We would like to believe that God can work miracles in his universe. But in a practical sense it is too big an idea to handle, and we're afraid of it. To accept that notion we would be forced to face life of a different and uncertain quality. We couldn't settle down behind conventional fences, phrases, and clichés. And so we drift into a lifestyle that is safer with the conventional, with the predictable, and the comfortable, and the manageable.

But regardless of how we feel about it—whether we believe it or not—the New Testament affirms that the same resurrected Christ who confronted the disciples behind locked doors and visited with Peter on the lakeshore is the contemporary Christ who confronts us *now,* to comfort and disturb, to save and to judge. What a staggering thought—especially when it is considered without all of the religious trappings that have accumulated throughout the centuries.

But how does he appear to us? I think that depends on the need. The Christ who appeared to his disciples before his ascension is described much differently than the Christ who appeared to John on Patmos. It was certainly essential that the disciples know beyond a shadow of a doubt that the risen Lord, speaking peace and empowering forgiveness, was the same person the Romans had impaled on the cross. Identification of the Christ of Easter with the Christ of Calvary, the King of Glory with the Man of Sorrows, is essential for the integrity of our gospel. The world does not need one more celestial phantom untouched by human agony any more than it needs one more tragic martyr to deepen our despair.

John on Patmos had no less real encounter, but it's clear that Christ's magnificence could not be handled for him by human conceptualization. And the same is true when the awesome and omnipotent Christ identifies himself to John, the writer of Revelation, as the same Jesus who was crucified on Calvary. Then, too, when Christ appeared to the Apostle Paul in the blinding light of the Damascus road, it was such an intense experience that he couldn't or wouldn't describe it.

I would certainly never say that these kinds of dramatic, miraculous, and visionary experiences don't or can't happen today. But I do believe they are not the normal manner by which Christ confronts us. Indeed, the final words recorded in John's Gospel commend those whose discipleship is based, not on external sight, as with Thomas, but on faith. Jesus Christ is present to us all the time—whether we see him or not depends on whether we *want* to see him.

There are three basic things which mark or characterize a personal encounter with Christ as I have experienced him. First, he makes me intensely aware of others or some Other. The attention is claimed by someone other than myself: Christ, a neighbor, a person in need. The center of the universe is experienced outside of me; there is a greater "whole," a higher degree of consciousness and personhood around me. Reuel Howe says worship is awareness, awareness of what's beyond the egocentric "I," awareness of these miraculous bodies and minds we have been given, awareness of others around us and their personhood. What marvelous gifts of creation they and we are! Worship is also awareness of the God who created all this and all that out there. It is to see the beauty around us from a glass of water to a candle to a leaf to a bird. All of this makes me want to clap my hands in joy that Christ is who he is, or I want to cry at the brokenness I see around me.

Second, in an encounter with Christ I am compelled to make personal and responsible choices. What I see and what I'm aware of creates the necessity for choice. And this arises from the contrast between the actual and the potential . . . between the way things are and the way they might be . . . between the state I am in and what I might be . . . between the situation others are in and the situation as it ought to be.

Such choices lead us to the third aspect of encounter: I am called forth. I'm compelled to take risks, to gamble past gains on a new initiative, to embark on what may seem to be a crazy adventure. I am called to give up what for the moment may seem self-satisfying to act on a compulsion to serve the Other through others. It seems that advance is always experienced through self-surrender of old habits and old securities. This is what is meant by "sacrifice." It is what the Bible means by "life through death," which Good Friday and Easter stand to affirm as God's way with his creation.

The disciples who had been cringing in fear behind the locked doors became new and changed men after this encounter with Christ. They "were filled with joy" instead of with terror; they were aware of an incredible purpose and mission beyond themselves, and the same process still goes on today.

A year or so ago Niel McManus came into my life. He had recently retired from the Foreign Service and moved to Austin with his ninety-year-old mother. Niel never told me why his wife stayed behind in Washington. He attended the Faith Alive weekend in our church and seemed deeply moved, especially during the altar call. Afterward he joined one of our groups.

But the experiences of that weekend and his new awareness of Christ brought him to the point of decision, and it was to move back with his wife. During the short time Niel was in Austin, though, the group he met with became deeply aware of him. A day or so after he moved out of his apartment but before he could leave for Washington, Niel became quite ill and went to the hospital. Now the members of his group were faced with choices—here was someone who needed them. And they visited him, prayed with and for him, supported him, and cared for his aged mother.

Now, these sacrifices and risks weren't necessarily earth-shaking, but they did involve an expense in time and thought in behalf of someone who obviously could not repay. Certainly, it involved time and thought which each person could well have used for pleasure or household chores. Niel recovered in time and went on to Washington. Shortly we received a request for the transfer of his church membership, and we heard that his son was to be married. But Niel died before this could happen. His death was a shock to all of us who knew him, but we were glad that before he died he had become more deeply aware of God and others—that he had made the choice to rejoin his family and had acted on that choice. It meant a great deal to us to know that during his final days in Austin he experienced genuine concern and unqualified love, which is indeed the essence of the incarnate and resurrected Christ in the Christian community. And we are glad that through him Christ appeared to some of us, making us aware of this stranger among us, and led us to choose to minister to him at some small self-sacrifice which ministry always involves.

This is how Christ appears to us 99 percent of the time—in ordinary, simple, everyday ways, rather than in dramatic and awesome events. The resurrected Christ walked with men on the road to Emmaus, he had a fish dinner with Peter, and I am convinced that all of us are invited to have such experiences and encounters *now,* in these closing years of the twentieth century. And if and when we do, we will come to know how Thomas felt when he was invited to touch Christ, and then responded, "My Lord and my God."

Live While You're Alive

Raymond C. Ortlund

"... I came that they may have life, and have it abundantly" (John 10:10).

To Exist but Not Really Live is a senseless waste and one of life's starkest tragedies. Yet millions of people find themselves doing precisely that. Like a hamster running furiously on the revolving wheel in its cage, so many of us are caught in the frenetic, give-and-take of life. We cover a lot of ground but really don't get anywhere. And worst of all, we've lost our zest; it's all pretty bland and tasteless. One person expressed it this way:

> People are faded. . . . They are not colorfast. In the downpour of calamity and the stress of human living the colors of life have faded into a sickly gray. If men are to get a sparkle, a buoyancy . . . they get it in Christ. Till then, life simply won't sing. Something lies songless within.
>
> I once had a canary that wouldn't sing until after it had its bath. Our souls are like that: Until we get a bath that cleanses away all fears, uncertainties, all guilt . . . the soul will not sing.

Now, when Jesus said, "I come that they may have life, and have it abundantly," he wasn't talking about a sterile, rat-race kind of existence. Life to him was not just going through the motions. He was intensely familiar with the hurts and frustrations and disappointments that penetrate every twenty-four hour period. Yet he insisted it shouldn't be that way.

Not long ago I was rushing through the sanctuary of our church in a hurry to get home when I noticed a person sitting in the darkened room. As I moved toward the still figure, I saw that is was a young lady and that

84

she was crying. Looking up through her tears, she said, "Pastor Ray, I am dirty. I'm no good." And she meant it.

We talked for a while; then prayed together. And it wasn't long before she experienced the cleansing and forgiveness which only God can give. Life began to make sense and have meaning.

Then, the moment I got home and was ready to settle down for a relaxed evening, the telephone jangled insistently. It was a friend from New Jersey: "I'm calling about my brother who lives in Pasadena. He's so disappointed and depressed. Can you help him?"

These are just two episodes among many, but they illustrate in living color the tragic fact that all around are thousands upon thousands of people who are depressed and utterly discouraged. Life just isn't what they had expected. They have an existence of sorts but need life.

What is real life?

No matter how often I hear it, I get a chuckle out of the story of the millionaire who died and in accordance with his instructions was to be buried in his gold Cadillac rather than in an ordinary casket. As the Cadillac was being lowered slowly into the huge grave, a bystander whispered in an awed voice, "Man, that's living!" Unfortunately, many people have been buried in high class who lived low lives. The question is well put in the Gospel account, "What will a man be profited, if he gains the whole world and forfeits his own soul?" An appropriate question—then and now.

But there is a life which has meaning—that doesn't wear out. It is eternal life. Jesus has it; he gives it: "I came that they may have life, and have it abundantly"

(John 10:10). Or, as this same verse is translated in *The New English Bible,* "I have come that men may have life, and may have it in all its fullness." What an offer! Not a frustrated, bland existence but fullness, completeness. And Jesus makes it clear that it is available . . . now.

This is such an amazing truth that it deserves a closer look—"I am come that you may have life." *Life and Christ are inseparable.* He *is* life. And when you have Christ, you have life . . . it comes from him. Fullness, completeness—this characterizes the life of the Christian; it is real life. Let's not be deceived, however. Real life is not carefree or trouble-free—a rose colored glasses kind of existence. That's phony and unreal. Life has its agonies and heartaches. It has its crosses as well as its Easters. Nowhere did Jesus promise to grease the skids so we can slip through life nonchalantly.

At the same time, real life is not living behind a mask . . . playacting as if everything is running smoothly on the surface while underneath, the turmoil is violent and erupts into physical and emotional ills of one kind or another.

Toward the end of Jesus' ministry he made this highly significant statement to his disciples in response to a penetrating question from Thomas, "I am the way, and the truth, and the life; no one comes to the Father, but by me" (John 14:6). First, he said, "I am *the* way." This is a definite statement that doesn't leave the door open for options. There is no going—no completeness —without *the way.* Next, he said, "I am the truth." There's no knowing without the truth. And, finally, he said, "I am life." There's no living without this life— his life. And life must come before either knowing or going.

86

Live While You're Alive

A new dimension

Two traveling men met for breakfast in a hotel dining room. They were greeted by a bubbly and gracious waitress who made them feel at home. She served them a delicious breakfast, and when they were finished, she walked to the door with them and said, "Have a wonderful day. And, gentlemen, *live alive all day.*" As they walked to their separate cars, they talked about that unusual comment: "Live alive all day." They were so intrigued that before starting their day's work they agreed to meet at the same hotel for breakfast the next morning.

Arriving at the hotel dining room the second time, the two men were greeted by the same friendly and outgoing waitress. As they were being seated, one of them said, "Yesterday, when we left, you told us to 'live alive all day.' That's a marvelous philosophy of life you have." She replied, "That isn't a philosophy of life; it is Christ. He's my answer. He brought me alive out of all kinds of sickness, darkness, and trouble. When I found him, I found life."

I think Jonathan Swift had this in mind when he made the interesting comment, "Live all the days of your life." In other words, when you're here, really go for life. There's just no good reason for going for half of life—a stale, dull routine; get hold of *life* and live.

Now, when Jesus said, "I am come that you might have life," I'm sure he wasn't referring to some superficial, self-generated kind of enthusiasm. We've all seen this and it has a hollow ring. Rather, it seems to me, there are four ways to describe the life Christ wants to give us.

First, I believe that Christ-life is *consciousness*. It is

awareness of the truth that when you received Christ, something climactic happened. As the blind man who was healed in the Scripture story said, "Once I was blind, but now I see." For the person who is alive in Christ, the senses are sharpened, consciousness is heightened. You become aware and sensitive to all of life.

But, it is also *contact*. You have made contact with God and there is an invasion of the Eternal in your life. What an awesome thought! You've made contact with the Creator of the universe, and he comes to be your abiding Friend.

And then Christ-life means *continuity*—life eternal. Jesus also said, "Verily, verily, I say unto you, he that heareth my word, and believeth on him that sent me, hath everlasting life." And this eternal life begins at the very moment you believe in Jesus. It's a life that doesn't quit. Death simply means a change of address.

Finally, this life is a *mystery*. Certainly there's no good explanation for physical life. What triggers the heartbeat which sends the blood pulsating throughout your body? No one has ever been able to describe and measure physical life—it is a mystery. And spiritual life is a double mystery. It's impossible to explain, but when we have life in Christ, we see and feel and hear and think differently. There is an expansive life inside, and suddenly we discover we've become elastic—God begins to stretch us out to previously unimaginable capacities.

Knowing Christ makes a difference

When Jesus talks about abundant life, I believe he is referring to a life of quality—a lifestyle which reflects newness and freshness and depth. It is an enlarged, vigorous, and vital life that doesn't come from our whipping it up but from God pouring it in. There's a vast difference between *life* and *abundant life*. It's like the difference between a baby bird that has a flicker of life but is still encased in the egg shell and that same little bird when it pecks its way out of the shell and breathes the air of the outside world—it is now free to grow and expand.

It seems to me that we have a great ·picture word in "abundance." It means to "abound" and stems from a picture word descriptive of waves flowing continuously onto an ocean beach. This is so symbolic of God at work. His provisions for a full and meaningful life are as ample and sure and endless as the motions of the tide which keep the waves rolling in their never-ending sequence. I like to believe that Jesus is really saying in this verse, "I want you to get out there in the surf and let the glorious, invigorating waters of my new life wash over you."

Nobility in Christ

While flying recently on one of our cross-country, commercial planes, I became absorbed in reading one of the airline magazines. An article entitled, "I Think I'm Going to Enjoy Nobility" really held my attention. It was the story about a commoner in England who had just been made a Peer by the queen. It seems that his first reaction was one of reluctance because of the responsibility that goes with the honor. However, as time passed and he experienced some of the benefits and luxuries of his new position, he changed his mind. This is indeed an apt illustration of the Christian. God offers us nobility in Jesus Christ. And while we tend to cringe at the awesome responsibility, we soon come to enjoy the abundance and fullness which saturates a life comitted to God.

Is your life a drag?

Are you fun to live with? On the surface that question might seem a bit flip, but, actually, it is intensely penetrating. It's a drag to be around so many people today—they're dull and no fun. I suppose this is one of the by-products of our highly organized, technological culture. We are excessively immersed in our narrow routines and become neurotic in trying to fit our lives into either round or square holes. And in the process we become plastic and sterile. The creative fun and zest is gone, and we're not much fun to be around.

Apparently, though, this is not a new phenomenon. Evidently Jesus ran into some pretty stuffy people— people who existed but didn't really live. For it was to them he said he came to bring a full and abundant lifestyle.

Unfortunately, far too many people seem to have a brand of Christianity which makes them miserable, and they in turn manage to infect those around them with misery. They're not fun to live with, and they're certainly not fun to be around. What a tragedy! But Jesus offers resurrection life with all its fullness and excitement and meaning. And the good news is: It is a miracle life that stretches and expands into newness and authentic joy.

Do You Believe This?

John A. Huffman, Jr.

Jesus said to her, "I am the resurrection and the life; he who believes in me, though he die, yet shall he live, and whoever lives and believes in me shall never die. Do you believe this?"
(John 11:25-26).

WHAT DIFFERENCE DOES the resurrection of Jesus Christ make? All the difference in the world! It equips us both to die and to live.

As we think together now, it is of primary importance to establish one essential fact: the literal, bodily resurrection of Jesus Christ from the dead. The One who cried out from the cross, "Father, into thy hands I commit my spirit," was dead. He was buried and sealed in a tomb. When the Apostles' Creed asserts that "He descended into hell," the concern is not with the location of Christ's activities in his death but to confirm once and for all that he literally died. He went to the place of departed spirits. Then he literally rose from the dead.

Now, the resurrection of Christ doesn't rest on unsupported assumptions. Luke affirms in his Gospel account that Jesus' resurrection is based upon "many infallible proofs." In a recent article Dr. Frank Gaebelein, former headmaster at Stony Brook School, presents a solid line of evidence: the empty tomb, the precisely laid out grave clothes, Jesus' numerous appearances to various people during the next forty days —Mary Magdalene, the two disciples on the Emmaus road, behind locked doors to the disciples when Thomas was absent, to the seven disciples on the shores of Galilee. And, finally, we read of his appearance to the group of five hundred, to James, and later to Paul on the Damascus road.

The very existence of the Christian church bears uncontestable witness to the fact that something happened to transform a broken and beaten group of losers into men and women who gave their very lives for the Christ whom they had seen and touched and felt in his resurrection power. Every Sunday brings affirmation of the living Christ. This is precisely why we no longer worship on the seventh day, the Sabbath. The day of Christ's resurrection was the first day of the week; this is the Lord's day. Jesus puts it plainly to the aged Apostle John, ". . . Fear not, I am the first and the last, and the living one; I died, and behold I am alive for evermore, and I have the keys of Death and Hades" (Rev. 1:17–18).

But more than all the factual data which we can accumulate to prove the literal resurrection of Jesus Christ is the very fact that he—right now, today—is in the business of changing lives. He is equipping people to live; he is equipping people to die. This was made clear in Jesus' words to Martha at Bethany on the occasion of Lazarus' death, ". . . I am the resurrection and the life; he who believes in me, though he die, yet shall he live, and whoever lives and believes in me, shall never die. Do you believe this?" (John 11:25–26). And after Martha's affirmative response to this penetrating question, Jesus walked resolutely to Lazarus' grave and called him back to life.

As we review the amazing movement of the intervening centuries from that awesome moment at the grave in Bethany to the present second, it becomes clear that everyone who has responded to the "do you believe?" question with Martha's answer, "Yes, Lord, I believe . . ." has experienced personal resurrection and new life.

The resurrection of Christ equips us to die

We are only equipped to live when we are prepared to die. That is an amazing paradox, isn't it? But right

now, each of us is suffering from a terminal disease—
we are in the process of dying. From that first moment
of breath, the dying process actually began. To recognize and accept this fact is not giving in to morbid
introspection; rather, it is acceptance of the reality of
life. And we're not really mature until we can confront
creatively the reality of our own death.

Elizabeth Kubler-Ross, a serious and reflective researcher on death and dying, says there are five stages a
person goes through in confronting the reality of his
own impending death.

The first stage is *denial.* "It can happen to someone
else, but not to me. Yes, I know death lies out ahead
somewhere, sometime, but not now. It just can't be
happening to me."

The second stage is *anger.* "I don't want to die. It's
not fair!" Resentfully, we shake our fist in the face of
life, in the face of God. Hostility and resentment roar
through every moment.

Next comes *bargaining.* "Okay, God, I guess I'm going to die. But, listen, if you heal me, I promise to serve
you faithfully. I'll go to church every Sunday and give
my money. Why, I'll even sacrifice my son to the ministry if that's what you want." I recall one woman who
asked God to let her live until her daughter's wedding.
She made it. Her doctor, in a spirit of comfort and sym-
pathy, commented, "God gave you your wish. You
attended your daughter's wedding." To which she responded, "Ah, doctor, but I have another daughter."
And so the bargaining goes on.

The fourth stage is *depression.* A gloom, a melan-
choly, settles over the terminally ill person. He crawls
into himself; his thoughts are introspective. Reality is
beginning to emerge. In a sense this is part of a responsible coping with the reality of death.

And, finally, there is *acceptance*. The facts have settled in. The person accepts the fact that he is going to die and there's nothing that can be done about it. Death becomes the one sure fact of life.

Now, the fact of Christ's resurrection from the dead releases us from ever having to deny or not accept the reality of death. This is because of four resurrection promises that trumpet an electric hope into the life of anyone who considers them seriously.

The resurrection promises life beyond this life. Jesus put it this way, "Let not your hearts be troubled; believe in God, believe also in me. In my Father's house are many rooms; if it were not so, would I have told you that I go to prepare a place for you? And when I go and prepare a place for you, I will come again and will take you to myself, that where I am you may be also. And you know the way where I am going" (John 14:1–4). And in 1 Corinthians 15 the Apostle Paul refers to Jesus as being "the first-fruits of them that are dead." His resurrection stands as evidence that life does not end with death.

The resurrection promises hope. Paul's ringing affirmation of hope is expressed in 1 Thessalonians 4:13–14, "But we would not have you ignorant, brethren, concerning those who are asleep, that you may not grieve as others do who have no hope. For since we believe that Jesus died and rose again, even so, through Jesus, God will bring with him those who have fallen asleep." The Christian need not be bogged down with sorrow as those who have no hope. It is true in a human sense we will miss that Christian loved one who has gone before, but we have the confidence that the separation is only for a time.

The resurrection promises reunion with loved ones in heaven. We are promised new bodies—spiritual

97

bodies (1 Cor. 15:44). And they will be recognizable. I believe the validation for this truth comes to us in the account of the transfiguration of Jesus. You recall that Moses and Elijah appeared and conversed with Jesus. They were readily identifiable to Peter, James, and John. Actually, we don't know very much about our future state of existence, but Jesus and the New Testament writers affirm its reality. And we can look forward expectantly to meeting our Savior and once again enjoying the presence of those we've loved here on earth.

The resurrection promises that we need not face the specter of hell. Jesus died to set us free from that ominous alienation from God. We are assured a place in heaven with Jesus Christ. But the same Bible which gives us that promise also points to a place of separation —hell—for those who reject the Savior, refusing to accept his gift of love and life made possible by the cross and resurrection.

The resurrection of Christ equips us to live

But the resurrection of Christ deals with more than the life after death. It has cataclysmic implications for our existence right now in this world. How?

The resurrection puts meaning back into life. One of the saddest memories I have is of a friend who really lost all interest in living. His wife divorced him and made it impossible for him to see his children. He drank too much, and in many ways there was an obvious weakness in his character. Yet he had a heart of gold. There wasn't anything he wouldn't do for a friend. And he dearly loved his children and wanted so much to see them.

I recall so well one night when he took a little cardboard plaque to a printer friend of ours and asked to have several copies made as a macabre present for some of his friends. It read: "For lack of interest, tomorrow has been cancelled." He went home that night, went to bed, but never woke up the next morning. No, he didn't commit suicide. Those of us who knew him best were convinced that his tomorrow had been cancelled simply for lack of interest.

In a March 10, 1975, editorial in the *New York Times*, Peter Marris, writing about "The Meaning of Grief," analyzes the contemporary American mood. He labels it one of grief: "Bereavement is therefore a crisis of meaning. Grief is the expression of an exhausting effort of reintegration, as much emotional as practical." He goes on to describe what we as a nation are going through with our economic, political, and international crises.

But some of us avoid this immediate lack of meaning by reverting to the past. We become extra-conservative, pretending to live in a bygone era that we're determined to resurrect into the present. Others of us are radicals who project into the future a new day, a new order that has meaning. Mr. Marris is convinced, however, that the answer is not in clinging to assumptions which deny the reality of change or in prescribing radical alternatives that deny the present. He calls for an integration of the best of the past within the inevitable change which is producing the future.

This may well be, but I'm convinced that Jesus Christ is the missing piece in the puzzle called life. Without him, you can *almost* get it back together. But then it shatters into the confusion of a million pieces. Jesus said, "I am come that you might have life, and have it more abundantly." He knows best how we should live. He ought to; he's the One who created us.

The resurrection offers authentic forgiveness. Even

as the sting of death is sin, sin is also the sting of life. And when Christ removed the sting from death, he also removed it from life. The March 9, 1975, *New York Times Magazine* carried a significant article about crime. The headline lead to the article read, "Intellectuals do not wish to be caught saying uncomplimentary things about mankind. But wicked people exist." True. But Christ's resurrection can remove that wickedness. It exposes us to the freeing catharsis of confession. Our guilt can be removed, and we can become whole persons: "If we confess our sins, he is faithful and just, and will forgive our sins and cleanse us from all unrighteousness" (1 John 1:9). No longer can Satan hold us in his clutches. We are a forgiven people.

The resurrection gives us strength to live. Christ said, "You shall receive power. After that, the Holy Spirit is come upon you . . ." Divine energy is ours . . . he gives us strength to live . . . his guidance is available . . . his direction is with us. Our faith and hope is not placed in a good man who died a martyr's death on a cross; it is in a risen Lord who walks with us now as an intimate friend.

Jesus Christ is alive today. He makes a difference in the life we live. He wants to equip us both to live and to die. He will, as we let him.

Tell Me About God

Reuben Job

For in him the whole fulness of deity dwells bodily, and you have come to fulness of life in him, who is the head of all rule and authority (Col. 2:9-10).

"WOULD YOU TELL me about God?"

Not sure I'd heard correctly, I bent down closer to the upturned freckled face of the nine-year-old little girl and asked, "What did you say,"

Again it came, "Would you tell me about God?"

I had heard correctly the first time. She was intensely serious. But I was a bit taken back because throughout the services leading up to Easter I had been trying to tell the story of God's amazing love as expressed in Jesus Christ. This little girl had heard me preach four times and still the question hadn't been answered to her satisfaction.

And so, even though her mother and father and brothers and sisters were waiting, little Anna and I had a quiet talk about God. We talked about Jesus and just what his death and resurrection meant to both of us right here and now.

As I reflected later on the poignant conversation, I was reminded that Anna's query is really the question of every person, irrespective as to how it is expressed. It has haunted humanity from the earliest moments of time. And even today, with the staggering array of technological advances which have produced gadgets in abundance to insure the ready supply of just about anything required for the good life, the deepest question, expressed or unexpressed, that seems to surface from the hearts of people everywhere is, "Would you tell us about God?"

Partial answers emerge from a wide variety of sources —from the physical world around us . . . from the sciences . . . from other Christians . . . from the sacraments of the church . . . from the Scriptures. But there is one place we can go for the complete answer: in the life, death, and resurrection of Jesus Christ. Here is indeed the ultimate response to the yearning of every person for an intimate knowledge of and relationship with God.

The Apostle Paul wrestled with the response to this question when writing to the early church, and he finally summed it up in the bold, sweeping statement, "For in him the whole fulness of deity dwells bodily, and you have come to fulness of life in him [Christ], who is the head of all rule and authority."

But how can we—you and I—respond to the Anna's in our neighborhoods, in our cities, in the world? I've pondered this long and hard, and it seems to me there are four specific ideas about God that point toward a clear answer.

God is greater than we can know or imagine

It seems that the world is actually getting too big for God. Our newspaper writers and television commentators spew out volumes on the crises of the times —a fluctuating and unstable economy where the Dow Jones refuses to respond in the normal patterns . . . ecological imbalances which threaten to permanently spoil the good earth and atmosphere . . . critical tensions which jeopardize peace in the Middle East, Asia, and the Third World . . . the unprecedented population explosion . . . energy shortages that point toward a complete revision of our lifestyle . . . a world food shortage which is taking a dreadful toll of human life through starvation. Our technology has conquered many of the mysteries of space, but we are failing miserably in meeting the physical and emotional needs of people in our country and around the world. It is obvious that with all our sophistication we are failing, and so we begin to wonder whether God can cope with the late twentieth century complexities. We know we can't. But can God?

This question must inevitably force us to a fresh look into the New Testament. And in the Gospels we find Jesus telling us about a God who *is* adequate for any need or task. He set free the oppressed; he gave bread to the hungry, healed the fractured, provided wholeness to splintered minds and hearts, breathed life into the dead. In the Gospels we hear this same Jesus calling God Father and are amazed that he invites us to do the same. Jesus tells us about a God who is too great to be pushed away, who is greater than the pain which seems to contradict him. Here indeed is a God who is greater than any creed, any church council, any theologian's lofty ideas, any denominational or sectarian limitations. Jesus points to a God whose power brought together an ordered universe and who is still creating in ways totally incomprehensible to our human minds. And at the same time he is a God who cares about the little things—a sparrow's fall, questioning children, trees that bear fruit, grass that dries up.

Yes, Jesus illuminates a God who is greater than we can ever know or imagine—one who defies human reasoning. He is forever above and beyond us.

The Apostle Paul, with amazing perception and understanding, caught a glimpse of this truth when he wrote, "O, the depth of the riches and wisdom and knowledge of God! How unsearchable are his judgments and how inscrutable are his ways! For who has known the mind of the Lord, or who has been his counselor? Or who has given a gift to him that he might be repaid? For from him and through him are all things. To him be glory forever." John Bennett affirms this awesome truth as he says that there are times when the very first word to be uttered about God is not love, not personality or greatness, but mystery, majesty, and transcendence.

And yet, when we want to know what God is like, we turn naturally to the Carpenter of Nazareth. For it is from him we learn that the world is not bigger than God . . . the world is just bigger than our idea of God, and we have to stretch and climb. With this blazing affirmation we can stand with confident assurance even in the shadow of the cross, knowing that truth, righteousness, justice, mercy, love, and life are not destroyed by the crucifixion. Rather, they are resurrected to new life and multiplied in countless ways.

God is near and approachable

Years ago when Debbie, our oldest daughter, was just a little girl, she illustrated this nearness and approachableness of God in a remarkable way. It was Sunday evening, following our family prayer time, and we were tucking her into bed. She was sort of hugging herself under the covers, and with dancing eyes she asked, "Do you know what I'm going to do when I see God?" Responding to her exuberance, we said, "No, what are you going to do?" And I'll never forget her answer, "I'm going to run up and give him a big hug and kiss."

Now, you may say that is just a child's theology and a conditioned response. Possibly so. I'm convinced, though, in this instance that her child's theology is laden with truth. For we must always balance the majesty and mystery of God—his otherness—with his

107

nearness and approachableness. The New Testament and Christian experience indicate that God's wooing, brooding, and searching Spirit is never far from any of us. The Psalmist echoed this eternal truth when he wrote, "Whither shall I go from thy Spirit? Or whither shall I flee from thy presence? If I ascend to heaven, thou art there! If I make my bed in Sheol, thou art there!" (Psa. 139:7–8).

One of the names given Jesus is Emmanuel: God with us. He is always near and approachable. This is one of the great affirmations of our Christian faith. And we see Jesus with all kinds of persons. He won't let any barrier of economy, class, caste, race, religion, or belief shield him and keep him from persons. In the Gospels we see him with little children, parents, fishermen, farmers, professors, prostitutes, tax collectors, shepherds, lawyers, doctors. In every instance he demonstrates that Almighty God is approachable and near. The crucifixion did not change that, and the resurrection simply underscores it.

Tex Evans, in his book entitled *Life Is Like That,* tells a remarkable story about Mr. Gentry, a leader in the community where Tex served as a student pastor in a small Methodist church. Tex noticed that whenever he walked past their house, Mr. Gentry was always whistling while he worked in his lush garden with its brilliantly colored flowers and green vegetables.

One day in a conversation with one of his own parishioners, Tex mentioned his curiosity about old Mr. Gentry and asked why he always whistled so loudly while working in the yard. His friend suggested that he stop by and visit Mr. Gentry and find out for himself. So, a few days later he opened the garden gate and introduced himself to the retired gardener. During the conversation Tex glanced up and saw an elderly woman sitting placidly on the porch in a wheel chair. Later he trumped up his courage and asked Mr. Gentry why he whistled so steadily and loudly, and then a beautiful story unfolded. Tex learned that the elderly woman was crippled and blind—Mr. Gentry whistled for the benefit of his wife. He wanted her to know that he was nearby, that she wasn't alone. He wanted her to know that he was mindful of her and that he wouldn't leave her; he was available and would go to her the moment she called.

Tex Evans goes on to say God is like that. He knows about us and is concerned for us—he won't leave us. God always gives us signs and songs in the night, in the midst of our own darkness, to assure us that he is present.

God offers the gift of himself to us and that gift brings countless rewards

Through Jesus Christ God offers the gift of himself to us. Imagine! Almighty God, the creator and fashioner of the universe is actually here with us now, cares deeply about both our joys and hurts, and is approachable.

The first sermon Jesus ever preached was in his home town synagogue. It's interesting to note that he didn't take this occasion to unwind a hefty theological discourse to impress his family and former neighbors. Rather, he dipped back into the ancient prophets and breathed a strange, new life into a few words from Isaiah 61: "The spirit of the Lord is upon me, because he has anointed me to preach good news to the poor. He has sent me to proclaim release to the captives and recovery of sight to the blind, to set at liberty those who are oppressed, to proclaim the acceptable year of the Lord."

Here, indeed, was the awesome message of salvation. Jesus didn't come to condemn, but to save: Good news to the poor . . . release to the captives . . . recovering of sight to the blind . . . liberty for the oppressed. Here God offers himself at the point of need, whatever and wherever it is. And that is what the New Testament is all about—this is the central truth of the Christian faith.

About a month after that first conversation with Anna, I received a letter from her. The last paragraph of that letter revealed just how easy it was for Anna now to believe in God's saving power: "Mr. Job, I have a big favor to ask. Please pray for my friend Bev. Bev's family is breaking up. Her mother and father are getting a divorce this summer, and Bev is scared. She needs your prayers."

I suppose there are those in these "enlightened" times who would label Anna's faith as woefully naïve. But it is the faith reflected in the New Testament. Whatever the chains which bind us at this moment . . . whatever the burden that is pressing us down . . . whatever the particular prison that has closed us in . . . whatever is smothering us . . . whatever blindness that has cut off our ability to see a way through; God through Christ offers himself, his saving presence, and his power to us. It is his gift.

My boyhood was spent on a farm in North Dakota. Every member of our family worked very hard. The times were not easy, and the few toys we had were handmade. My favorite was a slingshot. I remember when I got my first one. Dad had whittled it from the crotch of a cherry tree limb. The rubber bands were cut from an old, discarded inner tube, and the leather for the sling was from the tongue of an old boot. When dad finished it, he warned me against aiming at windows, persons, animals, and birds.

Most of the time I heeded his warning, but now and then I took secret joy in letting fly at the rump of an old cow that insisted on lagging behind the rest of the herd. And when no one was looking, I got back at an old buck sheep whose sole aim in life seemed to be in butting me from behind when I wasn't looking.

But I'll never forget one balmy summer evening when I was lounging along in a back pasture, dreaming dreams and enjoying the bird sounds which punctuated the stillness. Without aiming in any particular direction, I pulled back and released a flat stone from my slingshot that whistled off into the twilight. A moment later I heard the startled cry of a bird as it fluttered crazily to the ground. Looking down at the still form, I was crushed and frightened—sick to my stomach.

I ran back to the house, slipped inside quietly, and climbed into the security of my bed. But it wasn't long before I was crying, heartbroken. I had killed a bird. Feelings of guilt and remorse blanked out everything else, and I knew my father would be terribly disappointed.

Within a few moments I heard his steps and then he was sitting on the edge of the bed. I remember crawling up into his arms as the story gushed out. There I found comfort, forgiveness, and peace. And he assured me that tomorrow would come, there would be new opportunities to be responsible with all that had been entrusted to me, including the slingshot.

For me, at least, this story is a poignant reminder of the forgiveness, comfort, and peace that comes from God through the gift of his wholeness and salvation.

The Gift of Easter

God sends us out in mission to others

When we take the name Christian, we inevitably take upon ourselves the mission of Jesus: healing the sick, releasing the captives, helping the blind to see, offering good news to the poor, working for the liberation of all persons. In no way are these optional provisions. Rather they are the very stuff of the Christian's day-to-day bumps with life.

At no time has God invited his children to withdraw from the world. He hasn't stopped the world and instructed us to get off. Instead, he sends us in mission deep into the heart of the world. And it is there that we work and struggle and rejoice as God's special people, ministering to the hurt and brokenness that is tearing people up in our neighborhoods and towns. The gospel of the cross and the resurrection shouts the Good News of God in and with us—now!

It seems that whenever Christians come together, they talk to each other about God. This is a time of celebration and affirmation. But of even greater importance is our need, as Christians, to be talking with others about God. For after all, as we begin to know him, we discover personally that he is indeed greater than we could have imagined, yet he is closer than hands or feet. We come to understand, too, that while he offers himself to save and redeem, he also sends his people to help and to heal. This is the story of the New Testament; it is the story of the church; it is our story as Christians.

The Cost of Christ

David L. McKenna

*. . . and he who does not take his cross and
follow me is not worthy of me. He who finds his
life will lose it, and he who loses his life for my
sake will find it (Matt. 10:38-39).*

"Lent Will Not Cost Christians as much this year."

I had been driving alone, my mind preoccupied with many things, when my thinking was interrupted abruptly by this statement made by a radio newscaster. He went on to explain that the Pope had relaxed some of the restrictions on believers during the Holy Season.

But I was struck with the irony of this report because we know that the cost of genuine repentance has never been reduced. To the contrary, if there is a test which sounds the keynote for Christians during the Lenten season, it is found in the forceful words of Jesus when he said, "He who finds his life will lose it, and he who loses his life for my sake will find it." Taken literally, here is a promise in a paradox that is costly, non-negotiable, and irreducible. In fact, through this statement, Christ put before us one of the most far-reaching and soul-searching questions that we must ask, "What am I willing to give up in order to gain Christ?"

Our family circle is made up of four children, one daughter-in-law, one prospective son-in-law, and a fluctuating number of adopted college students, none of whom are particularly inhibited. Our dinner scene is usually a noisy and rollicking affair. But after the stale jokes and sibling jibes, most of the time the conversation turns to something more creative. At our last Christmas dinner we decided to characterize each member of the family by a single word or phrase. One of our teenagers became "You know" because of the frequency with which these words pop out in conversation. One of our younger members was called "Juice," since he wakes up and goes to bed every day with a glass of orange juice. Mom was immediately characterized by the words, "Let's relax and enjoy ourselves," as she always tries to get her hungry group to take time to chew as well as swallow. And dad . . . well, they had me pretty well pegged when they all chimed in together with, "Let's look at the options."

Obviously, this is not only a fun game but it also exposes pretty much just how we come across to other people. So let me pick up on the characterization which apparently fits me—an appeal to consider options. For I believe we see Christ talking about options in the words of our Scripture. Or to put it another way, if an economist were interpreting this verse, he might suggest that Christ was referring to "opportunity costs." What are you willing to give up in order to gain something else? Students, for instance, give up four years of earning power in order to attend college. Becoming a success in business demands a great deal of sacrifice and risk. Parents make enumerable sacrifices to give good things to their children.

But have we honestly and openly considered the cost we must pay if we are to gain Christ? What options confront us as we consider seriously the cost of losing our lives to gain him?

The call to be a Christian

Our first principle is so elementary that we might overlook it entirely: *We will have to risk self-love if we are to be Christian.* "Self" has taken on a new meaning today. At one time it was defined categorically in such vivid terms as hatred, jealousy, pride, or egotism. But this thinking promoted the idea that to lose one's self in order to gain Christ meant the regeneration from these overt and obvious acts of self-love. Today, though, "self" seems to have gone underground. This ties in with the complaint of Screwtape, the senior devil in the writings of C. S. Lewis when he says, "Great saints and great sinners are made out of the same stuff, but today we have only tasteless and flabby pretenders who give me indigestion."

What happened to the healthy sin of self? Karl Menninger, noted psychiatrist and author, is concerned with this question in his widely read book, *Whatever Became of Sin?* He says the root of the problem in modern society is a loss of the sense of sin. We turned sin into a *crime* by reducing the Ten Commandments and morality to thousands of laws. Now you sin before the state, not before God, so a fine or prison sentence will be your justification.

Conversely, Menninger suggests that we have made sin a symptom. The root of all evil is a miscoded gene, a warped childhood, or an emotional trauma. As a sedative for our sin, the word "maladjustment" has come into popular use. From another angle, Menninger also sees "collective responsibility" as a substitute for sin. We share the guilt of three hundred years of social injustice toward the blacks, and we are asked to accept part of the responsibility for the young murderer who was born amid the violence of the urban jungle.

It is certainly no wonder that Dr. Menninger calls for an awakened sense of sin. To clergymen he says:

> Preach! Tell it like it is. Say it from the pulpit. Cry it from the housetops.
> What shall we cry?

Cry comfort, cry repentance, cry hope. Because recognition of our part in the world transgression is the only remaining hope.

Then he identifies the root of the problem by quoting Arnold Toynbee:

I am convinced, myself, that man's fundamental problem is his human egocentricity.

Menninger and Toynbee can diagnose the disease of self-love, but they cannot cure it. It is interesting that Dr. Menninger concluded *Whatever Became of Sin?* with a chapter entitled "A Bluebird on a Dungheap." The idea presented here is that man's sin remains the stinking and polluting waste of his nature, but, hopefully, we will hear the bluebird's song on top of our depravity.

Self-love was the fundamental sin to which Christ spoke as well, but his remedy was not a bluebird on a dung heap. He stated clearly that we give the love of our heart, soul, mind, body, and strength to God without reservation if we want to gain abundant and eternal life. Here are new creatures in Christ Jesus, not bluebirds on a dung heap.

The call to be a servant

There is another cost to authentic discipleship: *We must risk our status to be servants.* When I was teaching Introductory Sociological classes, I used to present the theory that everyone must have someone to look down upon. The upper class looks down upon the middle class; the middle class looks down upon the lower class; and the lower class looks down upon an ethnic minority, usually black, but sometimes yellow or red. One explanation for the volatile frustration which boils up in the man on the bottom is that he has no one to whom he feels superior.

When Christ asks us to risk our status to be a servant, the question seems to come out this way, "Would you be willing to serve at the lowest frustrating level of human existence for My sake?" Does that question seem too radical or too theoretical? If so, read again these words of Paul:

> Let this mind be in you, which is also in Christ Jesus: Who, being in the form of God, thought it not robbery to be equal with God: But made himself of no reputation, and took upon him the form of a servant, and was made in the likeness of men: And being found in fashion as a man, he humbled himself, and became obedient to death, even the death of the cross (Phil. 2:5–8, KJV).

How far down is it from the glory of the Son of God to the likeness of man? How much farther down is it from manhood to servanthood? What is the distance between a humble servant and a crucified criminal? When Jesus died on the cross, every strata of human society could look down on him. But he chose to risk a status which began at the right hand of God and moved down the scale until he was numbered with the most despised men in his death. What a supreme cost to serve human need!

It was during a trip through New England with my family that we toured the replica of the Mayflower which is anchored in Plymouth Harbor. As I stooped under a beam in the cramped passenger section where the Pilgrims huddled together for more than two months, I recalled the moving account of the voyage in the historical novel entitled *One Small Candle*. The sea-toughened crew hated the Pilgrims because of their religious fervor and "puritanical" ways. During the first part of the voyage, the seamen cursed them, stole from them, picked fights, and brawled drunkenly in their presence. Then a plague broke out on the ship, and the less hardy Pilgrims were stricken first and many died. Soon, however, the disease spread to the crew, and many of them became deathly sick. When this happened, the unstricken seamen refused to go near their fellow crew members because the disease was so contagious. But the Pilgrims, who had survived, risked their lives and ministered to the desperately sick men who just a few days before had cursed them. This kind of courage and love made a lasting impression on the seamen. Many were saved from physical death and spiritual darkness through this selfless witness.

Each year at Commencement time, I try to emphasize this point to graduates: If their college careers are only tickets to admit them to a speedy social escalator, we have failed. But if they have heard the call of Christ, they will risk their status in order to serve. As we approach the tragedy and triumph of the cross in this season, can we risk any less?

The call to be a martyr

Our highest calling comes when Christ asks *if we are willing to risk our lives to be martyrs*. Certainly, no subject could be more unpopular for those of us who love life and want to live. But even as I write, I am reminded of an evening service which I attended in a Presbyterian church in Seoul, Korea. Fifteen hundred people filled the pews and testimonies were given by soldiers who had come to Christ that week. When the people sang with a gusto seldom heard in American churches, I was ashamed of my own joyless faith. After the service I asked the pastor what made the difference. Quickly, he responded, "You must remember that we are only one generation away from martyrs." Perhaps Winston Churchill had it right when he observed that the only trouble with Christianity in the twentieth century was that it hadn't bled enough.

But possibly the winds are changing. Recently Corrie ten Boom said that 60 percent of all the Christians in the world are being persecuted today. And Andrew Greeley, the Roman Catholic sociologist, predicts increasing hostility toward Christians in America as secularism and pluralism undermine our cultural heritage. When we visited Dachau recently, we viewed the history of the Nazi takeover in Germany which led to the persecution of the Jews. Three steps led to Dachau. At first they were told, "You cannot live among us as Jews," and the Nazis tried to convert them. When this failed, the Nazis said, "You cannot live among us," and they tried to expel them. This too failed, so the final solution to the Jewish question was , "You cannot live." And more than six million Jews were martyred who refused to be either converted or expelled.

How thankful to God we should be each day for our Christian freedom in America. At the same time we need to be very sensitive to the changes of thought and action in our national life. When a Henry Kissinger says off the record to Joseph Alsop that democracy is dead, we must be aware that our freedom as Christians could be declared null and void overnight. Then if we refused to be converted, we might be expelled. And if this failed, death could be the resolution of the Christian question. Remember, when the Apostle Paul wrote, "For me to live is Christ, and to die is gain," he was not a martyr with a strange, perverted, messianic complex fed by a sick mind. Paul had heard well the call of Christ, "He who loses his life for my sake will find it."

This is precisely why the Lenten season and all it stands for cannot be put on a bargain table. As we search for its full meaning in our lives, we must place ourselves and our commitment in the gain and loss columns of a spiritual equation and ask if we're willing to follow all the way to the cross. Perhaps you sense with me that:

> We gain pride, but lose the Spirit of Christ.
> We win comfort, but lose the edge of our witness.
> We rise in status, but miss human need.
> We save our lives, but withhold the gospel from others.

But, by vivid contrast are the words of an African who risked his life when he chose Christ. When he was asked to describe his feelings of what it meant to be a Christian—to be redeemed, he responded by saying,

> To be redeemed is
> To be awakened by the sound of a thousand trumpets
> And find it bliss
> To be alive in such a dawn as this.

To me, that is worth a world!

When Death Fails

Richard P. Langford

Men of Israel, hear these words: Jesus of Nazareth, a man attested to you by God with mighty works and wonders and signs which God did through him in your midst, as you yourselves know–this Jesus, delivered up according to the definite plan and foreknowledge of God, you crucified and killed by the hands of lawless men. But God raised him up, having loosed the pangs of death, because it was not possible for him to be held by it. For David says concerning him, "I saw the Lord always before me, for he is at my right hand that I may not be shaken; therefore my heart was glad, and my tongue rejoiced; moreover my flesh will dwell in hope. For thou wilt not abandon my soul to Hades, nor let thy Holy One see corruption. Thou hast made known to me the ways of life; thou wilt make me full of gladness with thy presence" (Acts 2:22-28).

What Is Life?

This is a question for which no person has found a satisfactory answer. And yet, with relentless insistence we struggle endlessly in our search for one. Glancing through a high powered microscope at the darting gyrations of those simple life forms in a drop of water, we look up in amazement and say, "This is life." Or in the spring of the year we wander across a hillside flooded with the color of wild flowers rippling in the soft air, and we say, "This is life." And for the avid outdoorsman who finds his way into the still back country, untouched by the pollution of the urban scene, the sight of a graceful fawn slipping through the trees or of a bounding bear cub cavorting along the edge of a rushing stream brings forth the exclamation, "This is life." But it is when we look at a new-born baby . . . or observe the miracle of a young child stretching toward maturity . . . or witness the struggle of a thinking person reaching toward identity and meaning—here in each of these cycles and moods we look up in wonder and say, "This is life." And if we could comprehend, even in our most vivid imaginations, a higher form than mankind, we most certainly would identify it as the ultimate life.

So our search for the answer continues—perhaps the most certain proof of life is what we feel surging within our own beings, and yet we struggle with the meaning of it all. A few years ago a song appeared on the scene that was good but too subjective and provocative to

126

really make it big. It told the haunting story of a little girl who was anticipating her first visit to the circus. Her emotions rode a high crest for several days, and finally the moment came . . . the air seemed alive with the sharp scent of sawdust and of trapeze performers, the shouts of clowns, the roar of lions in the ring, and the clop clop of galloping horses. And yet, as she walked out, the little girl asked, "Is that all there is to a circus?"

Time passed—she witnessed the excitement of a blazing fire, but turned away with, "Is that all there is to a fire?" Later she fell in love and was married, but after a time of disillusionment, she asked, "Is that all there is to love?" Finally, as the years passed, the little-girl-turned-aging-woman was afraid to die for fear that as she moved through the moment of death, she would ask, "Is that all there is to life?"

There are millions of people in the world today who feel exactly that way. We encounter them rushing frantically to beat the change from green to red in the traffic light . . . wandering in a semi-hypnotic state up and down the aisles of the supermarket . . . cheering wildly at a football game . . . staring unblinkingly night after night at the television screen. We know we're alive, but we always have the feeling that *life*—the excitement of living—is just around some corner up ahead wrapped up in a certain anticipated event. Then we round the corner and ask with a letdown feeling, "Is that all there is?" And ultimately we seem to reach the place where our rationalization for every disappointment is, "There are only two sure things in life—death and taxes."

Death—what an enigma . . . we define life by death as if we were certain that death was always the winner. It's amazing, isn't it, that whenever we attempt to define life, we always end with death as the boundaries. What a paradox!

However, deep within each of us is the haunting feeling that death may not be the end or the winner. There is the lurking suspicion that life is drawn from a higher, eternal source—it is not just self-existent. And somehow, life, even with all of its questions and dilemmas, may be a lasting gift—perhaps the trip through death may bring us face to face with the giver.

If it were not for that strange inner feeling, if we were sure that death is the end, we could then live life as one long party with no concern for responsibilities or consequences. But we're not certain, and the questions linger on.

The problem of life and death

The words of Acts 2:22–28 emerge from that kind of struggle. Peter is talking to the crowd in Jerusalem at Pentecost, just fifty days after the crucifixion of Jesus. Jesus had posed a serious threat to the people in that crowd, so they had him arrested, tried unjustly, and executed. A sense of satisfaction had swept the city then, for the troublesome preacher was out of the way. But then something happened . . . different people, individually and in groups, said they had seen him. And Peter's message was that death had failed.

You can be sure that in a city as small as Jerusalem this was a central topic for long and animated discussion. You see, there weren't the artificial diversions then which we have today that inhibit conversation. Doubtless the people struggled over what they heard. Was it truth? Or a lie? Had death failed? The dilemma posed by that question has gripped people of every generation. We struggle to *live;* we struggle *with* death.

A few years ago a doctor friend of mine who teaches at a medical school told me that the aim of medical science is to do away with morbidity and mortality—to eliminate sickness and death. And, certainly, great strides have been made in combating effectively so many of those killing diseases which have terrorized mankind from the beginning.

A superb example of the advances which have been made in the struggle with death was described in the February 1975 issue of *Readers Digest.* Linda Honicker, a college girl from Nashville, Tennessee, was told that she had leukemia. Her condition deteriorated steadily, and, finally, her doctor suggested that she be taken to the University of Washington Adult Leukemia Center where she underwent a bone marrow transplant. Linda almost died when the leukemic cells invaded her brain, but her young doctor fought valiantly to save her life—at one point he never left her bedside for thirty-six hours. But the transplant took, and Linda began the long and torturous path to recovery.

In time she was able to return home. Her father wrote, "On May 11, 1974—day 365 post-transplant—the Honicker family sat around the dining room table in Nashville and lit one candle on a huge cake, with happy tears flowing. They choked out a variation of an old song, 'Happy rebirthday, dear Linda!' For indeed Linda had been reborn a year ago to the day." And according to Linda's doctors, there is every medical sign that Linda has won her battle against leukemia. But, as with all of us, she is still in the struggle. No one can predict the future, but we know that out ahead lies the reality of death.

A few years ago a new play was written based on the story of Lazarus being called from the grave by Jesus. The author very graphically pictured some of the ways in which we handle the subject of death. He portrays Martha as the rationalist who comes to Jesus with a systematized set of beliefs about death. She knows that Larry, as Lazarus is called in the play, will rise again in the last day. She has a belief about an after-life, and she calmly accepts it all. Mary, on the other hand, is very emotional. She agonizes over the whole concept of death and is certain that if Jesus had just been there, he would have prevented Larry's death. She weeps and struggles.

The friends who see Larry after Jesus brought him back to life also struggle with the fact that Larry has come out of the grave. But the one arresting thing which you remember about the play is the appearance and attitude of Larry himself after the grave experience. There was a strange and wistful look in his eyes that made you wonder just what he had seen that caused him to look so longingly past this present life. The author implants the idea that while in the grave Larry had seen something the human eye cannot see, that he came to know something that this life at its best does not reveal and death at its worst cannot keep him from achieving. Then, too, Larry seems to be struggling with the notion that possibly death can fail, even though we tend to see it as the final victor.

The promise

In our Scripture lesson in Acts Peter affirms positively that death has failed. The argument is conclusive. Death could not hold Jesus Christ . . . for two basic reasons. The first burst through the words of prophecy which came from David hundreds of years before. It was a promise that the grip of death would be broken— by the promised One, the Messiah. And Peter had every reason to know what that promise meant. He had walked through the dark hours after the crucifixion with his stifling load of guilt. Then he came face to face with the risen Jesus and all earlier questions were answered. So, it was with boldness and confidence that Peter told the Pentecost crowd that "Jesus is alive. He had conquered death." Death had failed.

The people listening to Peter's great affirmation were very familiar with the promise of David's that the Holy One would not see corruption. It was their own prophecy which insisted that the Messiah could not remain in the grave. And to the Jews of Peter's day, the prophets were held in high regard—they were the confidants of God. He whispered into their souls by his Spirit; he shared his secret resolution of the future with them. Now Jesus had been raised from the dead in fulfillment of the promise.

That victory of Jesus over death has intense significance for us—you and me—now, for it brings us a touch of life and the complete confidence that death does fail. Recently, I visited in the hospital with a marvelous lady. Her face was lined with age and with the pain which had eaten most of the life out of her. The nurse roused her so we could talk briefly. After a few moments I asked if she would like for me to read a few verses of Scripture. Standing closely beside her bed, I read these words from Acts 2 and Psalm 16, "I saw the Lord always before me, for he is at my right hand that I may not be shaken; therefore my heart was glad, and my tongue rejoiced; moreover my flesh will dwell in hope. For thou wilt not abandon my soul to Hades, nor let thy Holy One see corruption. Thou hast made known to me the ways of life; thou wilt make me full of gladness with thy presence." As I read those words, a calm and beautiful smile crossed her face. It was as if she saw the reality of her own life in the One who had conquered death. It was as if the Lord Jesus came back and took her into his arms for the touch of life.

Power

But for Peter there was even a greater argument than that of the promise of Scripture: It was the character of Jesus. *He was the life.* He was the Prince of life— the very Source of life. Death could not define his life because he was the source of the power of life itself. William Barclay puts it well for us today, "A Christian is one who never forgets that he lives and walks with a risen Lord." It is this eternal truth which makes true celebration of life possible. By his word and his character . . . *Jesus is life.*

Our Call and Cross

George A. Buttrick

*And immediately he called them; and they left
their father Zebedee in the boat with the hired
servants, and followed him (Mark 1:20).
And he called to him the multitude with his
disciples, and said to them, "If any man would
come after me, let him deny himself and take up
his cross and follow me (Mark 8:34).*

This word "called": if someone said, "There's a call for you," you would go quickly to the telephone wondering if the call were casual or (as we say) serious. If your name were called over the loud speaker at a public meeting, you would instantly respond with a flutter of mind.

I

The call of Christ is in another dimension. It is heaven calling earth—person to person. The Old Testament tells of God calling this man and that— Gideon, Isaiah. The word "call" on the lips of Christ has that same authority. Charge Christ with presumption or egomania, the fact stands. Christ presented his claims, and then brooked no argument: the person called said "yes" or "no." *"Immediately"* he called them—imperiously as heaven's emissary. The scholars tell us that Christ probably never pointedly claimed the title "Messiah." If they are right, we understand why: The title had been traduced by Jews who wanted their own Caesar. But Christ *did* claim to be higher than Mount Sinai or any Law: "You have heard how it was said of old time, but I say. . . ."

But couldn't people volunteer to follow? Yes, and they did, not to become rabbis as with the students of Hillel, or philosophers, as with the followers of Socrates: for another mission. And what sifting when anyone did volunteer! One man offered, and Jesus

said: "I'm homeless. Do you want to be homeless?"
Another came with a good resolve: "But let me first
live out my father's last years": fair enough; it was an
obligation under the Jewish law. But Christ said, "Let
the dead bury their dead"! The harshest answer spoke
about a cross: "If any man would come after me, let
him take up his cross and follow me." He still speaks
that way. By comparison any word from Washington
is a cheap echo of an echo.

II

Then what is our cross? Not our sufferings. They
come for all of us and must be borne. Usually they defy
any neat explanation. But I mustn't say of my gimpy
leg: "It's my cross." It isn't. W. M. Clow said years
ago: "We are conscripted to carry burdens; we volunteer to carry our cross." Sure, we "take up" our cross.
The word plainly refers to the way Christ died. Crucifixion was then a Roman form of execution. Christ
was condemned by a Roman court. So we shouldn't
call Jews "Jesus killers," though their leaders played a
guilty part. But they were not guilty for being Jews.
Jesus was a Jew. So were his first disciples through
whom we learn of him. Had we been there what would
we have done? Remember: There was as yet no Easter,
no New Testament, no Church. We might have reck-
oned Christ a troublemaker. We live on the fortunate
side of Calvary.

*Then how come Jesus was crucified in a death so
shameful* that no Roman, however rotten, was crucified? Because of what Christ said and did. He *identified
with the poor,* while certain of our national leaders
warn that we are spending too much money on the

137

needy. They can always find money for the Pentagon, but cannot or will not provide work for the unemployed. Christ *identified with the captives*. He said, "I was in prison . . ." and that we either visit him or forget him. He *identified with the oppressed,* his compatriots under the Roman conquest. No, he refused to join the guerilla underground, and prophesied that they invited a bloodbath. Events justified him. But he stood with anyone who was denied a rightful freedom. He *identified with the wicked,* not ever to share or condone their guilt, but to win them to a joyous life. There's a final term: He *identified with the abandoned.* If you do not "get" that word, think of your own inevitable death and you will understand: "My God, my God, why have you forsaken me?" All these were Christ's friends, the strangest list of important folk our planet has ever known.

We should add that Christ lived this way under the same authority by which he called people. This way of life, he was sure, is God's will, nay, God's nature, for "God is love": *this kind* of love. Young people now say, "Love is God," which is better than saying that cash or power is God. But what kind of love? Not love as romantic, selfish sex! Not even love as "loyalty." Loyalty to what or whom? Not loyalty as mutual obsession. How little we know about Christ. He shared every form of hurt, and so died in degradation. We decorate the Cross. We try to domesticate the Cross. No way! It's a gallows, the bottom rung of the ladder of shame.

III

Then how come so gentle a Christ was crucified? Have you ever asked? Because if you stand with the poor, never pretending they are saints, you offend the rich; they think you are a "radical." If you plead for the captives, you run foul of the law-and-order group who won't admit that law is unequally administered and that millions on our planet live in dingy disorder, and that our penal system turns criminals into worse criminals. Continue the list: If you stand with the oppressed, you tangle with the oppressor, you trouble his conscience (if any) and threaten his power. If you plead for the wicked, the righteous (if any), are horrified, they suggest that you are guilty by association. As for the abandoned, let's read the book "On Death and Dying," but let's not really confront our own death.

So the Temple saw Christ as blasphemer. They were right on their terms. He broke the ancient Jewish law, e.g., by healing folk on the Sabbath. He called men by God's own authority. He consorted with sinners. He ignored the line between Jew and Gentile. If his way prevailed, Temple and synagogue would disappear or take a new form. Had we lived then we might have opposed him. We don't oppose him now; we make a tame plastic Christ, and then follow. I've heard of a certain church, with blacks encroaching, which was asked if its excellent but almost empty facilities were available for a community center. The membership voted heavily against the proposal—for obvious reasons. An angry parishioner wrote condemning the minister for pursuing these will-of-the-wisps. So Jesus got a new title: He's a will-of-the-wisp. That's a worse slur than blasphemer.

To the Empire Jesus was a rebel. True: Jesus refused to join the guerilla underground, the Zealots. He warned that they were inviting a bloodbath, which came to pass. Physical force provokes an answering

139

force plus hatred. So Jesus was accused of lacking patriotism, while Barabbas, probably a Zealot, was popular. But Jesus had no part with the oppressor: "Their great ones lord it over them: it shall not be so among you." Jesus organized no political party and proposed no economic system. His kingdom was "not of this world," not timebound, not corruptible. But Jesus was obviously a potential focus of insurgence. Suppose he should gather the crowd. He did for a time. So to the Empire Jesus was a rebel.

Note this, even though we don't wish to note it: Jesus died a public death. No, not because he was a "radical," but because in love he made common cause with the dispossessed, and so offended the mighty. He did not live with the poor and keep his mouth closed; he grappled with "the establishment." He said that the Temple, seat of his domestic government, was doomed. As for the Empire, he said of Herod, who was more powerful than Pilate, "Go tell that fox . . ." That crack did not go unnoticed. Our revivalists pretend that sin is a private affair: "Don't drink, don't swear, don't cheat, don't steal." There's no sin in government, or in great corporations, or in military conquest. Then revivalists kid themselves that "changed people change the world." They don't. They join the ranks of the entrenched. They even make alliance with the centers of power. Faith in Christ is *both* private piety and public courage. Our cross is to follow Christ.

IV

Question of questions: How could our Faith survive the bottommost degradation of that gallows? Would you like to go through life pleading with your neighbors to follow a criminal? Would you like to say, "He hung on a gibbet while the crowd jeered"? No church could have survived such a creed, let alone be born in it. But that was not the message of the apostles. They said in triumph, "He was raised from the dead!" There are many evidences for the Resurrection. Evidences: no proof, for proof leaves no options, no room for venture. The central evidence is that a criminal conquered! We try to forget the criminal, and can't forget. He is surer to me than I am to myself. He is my only comfort and no comfort at all—my only comfort because he has made common cause with my failures to redeem them by God's authority, no comfort because he calls me to take up my cross and follow. But no comfort is yet love and victory: He was raised from the dead. The Cross is the way to eternal life.

So the New Testament always links Calvary and Easter. "God forbid that I should glory save in the cross of Christ my Lord." But that, you say, stops at Calvary. Oh no, it stops at Christ my Lord. When Israel translated its Hebrew Scriptures into Greek because Israel then lived in a Greek-speaking world, the word they used for Jehovah (Jahweh), the chief Old Testament name for God, was the Greek *kyrios:* "Lord." The name Christ itself means "Savior-King." "Christ my Lord": not "Christ who seemed to be Lord before he was hung," but "Christ now because he was raised from the dead." So Paul, thus glorying, carried his cross, in and out of jail, following Christ, living in love for the disinherited, and again and again running foul of "the authorities." Once in a while our hymns catch the glory:

> "Rich wounds yet visible above
> In beauty glorified."

That angels can see the wound-prints of Christ which now glow like stars!

V

So Christ calls his Church. The call is still imperious and utter lowliness, the voice of God who in his Son is ready to die on a Cross. Did Christ intend the Church? Well, he "chose twelve," to continue the covenant with the Twelve Tribes—in the "New covenant in My blood." They were a strange twelve: One was a Zealot, member of the guerilla underground; another was a tax-gatherer, a Jew who had so demeaned himself as to collect Roman taxes; another was Peter, who leaped before he looked and tried to make Jesus a nationalistic Messiah; and another, Thomas, was a doubter to the end. Christ could find their like, blundering and wonderful, down any street, in any church. He gathered them, all but one, into his own strange love for third-degree citizens. Does his mission make our churches "weak"? Yes, by the world's reckonings. But why forget the Resurrection? Why flout the brave insight of the New Testament (what a book!): "The foolishness of God is wiser than men, and the weakness of God is stronger than men." So Christ calls his Church.

He calls you and me. The revivalists are half-right: Our sins *are* private, but our worst sin is failure to protest massive corporate sins (war, poverty, unemployment, racism) for the sake of the dispossessed. The revivalists *are* half-right: Faith in Christ is personal piety, for to him, prayer was not something added; it was his main endeavor. But they are half-wrong: Faith in Christ is public courage, a grappling with the "mighty" for the sake of the disinherited—at cost of a cross. So revivalism, cluttering the airways, is a miasmic cowardice, while it rakes in the coins. The modern instance? History gives many examples, but possibly the most recent is found in South Korea. Here one group brags of the millions who attended a rally (the cult of numbers), but President Park, a nasty little despot, is on the platform even though he imprisoned over a hundred Catholic priests and Protestant missionaries whose sole crime is opposition to his tyranny. Imagine Jesus in South Korea? Would he be on the platform or in jail? John Chancellor, braver than our pulpits, recently hailed the Korean newspapers that have defied Park.

VI

So the Cross for you and me is private discipline and public risk. But it is all for his sake—who was hung as a criminal and raised from the dead. We can't side-step the call. If we dodge it here, we shall meet it hereafter, for that Gallows-Man is now Lord of heaven and earth. "If any man would come after me, let him deny himself and take up his cross and follow me."

You Go First, Lord. I'll Follow.

Charlie W. Shedd

*And go quickly, and tell his disciples that he is
risen from the dead; and, behold, he goeth before
you into Galilee; there ye shall see him: lo, I have
told you (Matt. 28:7).*

WHEN WAS THE LAST TIME you found yourself speechless? A sunset? Moon over the water? Or was it a people-experience? Some high moment, or low? Somebody got to you. It hurt, but you knew the best answer was no answer. Whether it was beautiful or otherwise, there you were without words.

That's how it is with me at Easter. I know what Easter means, and I'm glad I do. I even believe the Resurrection is doctrine number one of our faith. Christ is alive. God is in charge. And here I am with my little tin trumpet.

Gabriel, lend me your horn!

There are high notes here my bugle cannot blow. This message deserves the very best, including angelic choirs. Open those upper windows and let us hear it like it is. "Praise Him all ye heavenly hosts."

Whenever I'm in a predicament like this, I back off and say a prayer: "Lord, this is much too much for me. Here are your people. They have come to worship, and you know how it is. This well is deep, and I have little with which to draw. Give me a word straight from you. For me. For them."

When I pray that prayer, I'm often led to some small part of the passage. One little phrase which I can understand. A single text for focus. Here it is in Matthew 28:7, ". . . behold, he goeth before you . . ."

Does He?

That's a good thing you're telling me, angel. And some of my friends admit they have the same problem.

So easy to get six jumps ahead of our Lord. "Hurry up, God. All these things to do and not enough time to do them."

Worry, worry, rush, rush, rush. So, thanks for reminding me there is a right order. For life to be right with the risen Christ, he must go first and I follow.

I

"Who will roll away the stone?"

Poor women. Tied up in knots. Beat. All the pastel colors gone now from their sunrise. Hear them moaning on their way to the tomb, "Who shall roll away the stone from the door of the sepulchre?"

Good question! Tombs were carved in the hillside with no access except the doorway. Over the doorway they rolled a massive stone. If you have seen this arrangement, you know there is a trough in front of the tomb. They wet it down or oil it to make for easy rolling. But even then it would take several men to move the thing. So what are a couple of women with a stone that formidable? Yet here it is in the Book. Mark 16:3–4: "And when they looked, they saw that the stone was already rolled away."

Isn't that just like God? He goes ahead to handle our worries. But that isn't all. He does even better than we can imagine. He sends his angel. Sometimes the angel is a person. Then again, a circumstance. Or he gives us extra time and extra strength we didn't know we had. If only I could learn to trust him. But there I am, so often running down the road and calling him to follow me. And the further ahead of him I go, the more I worry.

Randy is a high school senior, and he's a winner.

First string linebacker. Two years ago his father was transferred. Randy wanted to stay behind to finish his schooling. His mother and dad said, "No way!"

So he went, dragging his feet. Randy was sure his world was caving in. How would he ever make friends like those he was leaving? What if he didn't make the team at his new school? Why couldn't his folks understand?

Comes now this letter from Randy with one short paragraph I thought you'd like. Since we had been close friends, he's sharing the good news with me:

> "It looks like I'm going to make all-conference. And that means I can go to State. But the really neat thing is Billie Jean. I met her right after we came here. And there is no way I can tell you about her. She's the greatest!"

Mothers. Fathers. Businessmen. Housewives. Doctors, lawyers, preachers, teachers, farmers, clerks, and pumpers of gasoline. Old, young. Every size, every shape. Every person on earth needs Easter. This is the word: "He goeth before you."

II

If we practice living this way in the little things, here's another Easter note of good news.

No need now to fear death.

I don't want to be morbid, but this is a fact. One day every one of life's love-ties will be ended. No exceptions. Strut as we will, the time comes. We, too, find ourselves in a room with the shades drawn and people talking in whispers. Death takes even the proudest. It points its bony finger our way and says, "Your turn."

What will we do?

We'll do just fine, thank you, if all our life in little things, we've been taking the angel at his word . . .

"Behold, He goeth before you."

On a radio show years back I heard one beautiful witness. It was a secular program, one of those "men on the street" affairs. The announcer had gone to a busy corner and today he was talking with girls. These were high schoolers on their annual "sneak day" to the big city. Silly. Some were downright giddy. Giggling. Laughing. Whispering. Clowning. Except for one girl. She was the epitome of perfect poise. A true lady, keeping her cool and calmly saying what she thought.

The announcer was obviously impressed. Plus grateful that his show wouldn't totally bomb. So he asked her, "How come you're so calm? You must have been on radio before."

She hadn't. Then he pushed for an explanation. And she had one. "I don't get scared like my friends do and the reason is my mother. When I was eleven, she died. That night she called us in and told us, 'I want you girls to know I'm going to die, but I'm not afraid. The Lord promised to prepare a place for me. And I believe him. If you will remember this, you won't be afraid to die. And if you're not afraid to die, you don't need to be afraid of anything.' "

So why should she fear a microphone?

Life gets heavy. Time closes in. There's been a death in your family and you're lonely. Your body begins to give out. Aches. Pains. Is something moving in on you? Tragedy? Death and the hard things seem so big and we are so little.

Then here comes the Easter angel to tell it like it is. God can split little tombs or big ones. He can smooth the road, light the way, handle our problems before we get to them. He's the Lord of those happy surprises.

How does He do it? I don't understand. I can't comprehend Easter, nor even his every day love.

But I can comprehend this. The Easter secret for life at its best is to pray, and keep praying . . .

"You go first, Lord. I'll follow."

A Revolution of Faith

Floyd Thatcher

Jesus declared publicly: "Whoever believes in me believes not in me but in the one who sent me, and whoever sees me, sees the one who sent me. I, the light, have come into the world, so that whoever believes in me need not stay in the dark anymore . . . I have come not to condemn the world but to save the world" (John 10:44–47).

THE MOST AUDACIOUS revolutionary movement in human history was triggered by the life, death, and resurrection of Jesus Christ. And as during the birth pangs of every revolution, when the status quo is threatened and the stirring of change is felt, comfortable people—the establishmentarians—were first amazed and nervous. Next came hostility and anger, and finally, there emerged the will to eliminate the threat by whatever means was necessary—to kill him.

This progression is easy to trace in the Gospel story as we first see people being impressed and amazed at the action and teaching of Jesus: ". . . his teaching made a deep impression on the people" . . . "A feeling of awe came over the crowd" . . . "They were utterly and completely dumbfounded" (Matt. 7:29, Matt 9:8, Mark 6:52).

But for the crowds, this soon changed: "After hearing it, many of his followers said, 'This is intolerable language, How could anyone accept it?'" . . . "It was because he did things like this on the Sabbath that the Jews began to persecute Jesus" . . . "The world cannot hate you, but it does hate me" (John 6:60–61, John 5:16, John 7:7).

Finally, their anger peaked and the will to murder surfaced: ". . . and the chief priests and scribes were looking for some way of doing away with him . . ." ". . . he could not stay in Judaea, because the Jews were out to kill him . . ." "From that day they were determined to kill him" (Luke 22:2, John 7:1, John 11:53).

154

A Revolution of Faith

And crucify him they did. Both the pagan Roman soldiers and the pious, traditionalist, religious Jews were convinced that the revolution was over. Now the common people who had been attracted to the radical and troublesome Nazarene would settle down once more behind their barricades of apathy. But it wasn't to be. On the third day there was the missing body. Then rumors filtered in of people who had seen the risen Jesus. And weeks later the fuse was ignited on the Day of Pentecost which released revolutionary forces of faith into the Roman world. A revolution of "light"—the Light of God—had the world in its grip and nothing would ever be the same again.

It wasn't. The cowering and frightened Peter who had denied his Lord profanely became the bold preacher at Pentecost. He was so persuasive that "They were convinced by his arguments, and they accepted what he said and were baptized. That very day about three thousand were added to their number" (Acts 2:41). What a dramatic change!

At the murder of Stephen for his faith it is written that "Saul entirely approved of the killing . . . Saul then worked for the total destruction of the Church; he went from house to house arresting both men and women and sending them to prison" (Acts 8:1,3). But following his confrontation with Jesus Christ on the Damascus road a climactic change occurred, and he became the mighty preacher and missionary whose primary theme, "Jesus is the Son of God," spread like a gasoline fire across the world. Saul, now Paul, was to experience beatings, imprisonment, shipwreck, and finally death at the hand of an executioner's axe for his faith. What a dramatic change! And yet it is this spirit which held the early Christians in a vise-like grip and propelled them into society with a force and flavor that demanded attention and provoked change.

Such has been the pattern of Christian history—bold men and women ignited by Christ's love and power have become fearless agents of change. But it has never come easy and often at high cost. When a Luther or a Knox or a Wesley moved out of a sequestered existence and began to exercise a vital faith in the everyday affairs of life, changes occurred—lives were transformed into a caring concern for the hearts and welfare of people and of nations. If some were enslaved to other people or were oppressed by a system or a set of ideas, the winds of a fresh revolution of faith blew in the changes which set people free. There have always been the few who took seriously the affirmation of Jesus: "In the world you will have trouble, but be brave: I have conquered the world" (John 16:33).

But today we suffer from a strange fatigue. The pace of scientific, technological, and social change during the past thirty years has us reeling—we've lived through almost more than we can absorb. And so we've become blasé and seem to have lost our sense of wonder. I recall so well that great moment in my own life when I stood in the V.I.P. stands at Cape Canaveral with my eyes glued to the Apollo 10 spacecraft a mile or so away, perched atop its Saturn rocket on the launch pad. Then came the moment of ignition and lift-off and with tears streaming down my face I watched that spacecraft move up in a blaze of fire and staccato thunder until it raced out of sight. And then as the craft plunged downrange at an unbelievable speed, the amplifying system crackled with the reassuring voice of Commander Tom Stafford, whom I had met and talked with just a few months before. All was well and that historic rendezvous with destiny a few miles above the moon's surface paved the way for the dramatic landing of Apollo 11. It wasn't long, though, before in the minds of most people such events attracted little attention and the space program suffered severe cutbacks for lack of interest and money.

To me, this is but a symbol of our strange mood. Our spirit of change and adventure suffers from a short attention span. Fatigue seems to draw us back into a narrowness, a satisfaction with the status quo, which we don't want disturbed or we may find ourselves being called to an effort or commitment we're unwilling to make.

Far too many of us move in and out of each day with prefabricated prejudices and assembly line attitudes. Other than what it takes to fulfill the routine of a job, lob a tennis ball across the net, or hit a small, white ball on the golf course, we seem to have little energy left for the excitement and stimulation of life—unaware of the fact that narrowness is within ourselves, not in our circumstances and surroundings.

Several years ago, writing in *Saturday Review,* Dr. Franklin Murphy put it this way, "The American society now is confused, insecure, and, from time to time, destructively irrational. We wonder if we have lost the capacity to manage ourselves and find the future."

But find the future we must. And as Christians, we will when we recapture the revolutionary vitality of Jesus Christ, who said, "I, the light, have come into the world, so that whoever believes in me need not stay in the dark anymore" . . . ". . . but be brave: I have conquered the world."

The resurrection of Jesus Christ on that first Easter

morning meant that death was conquered once and for all, and it was indeed the fulfillment of his promise in John 10:10, "I have come so that they may have life and have it to the full." Here is the Source for excitement and anticipation for change that will move us into each day and season with a profound caring about what happens to people around us. Our spirits will be intensely uneasy and uncomfortable as long as one person anywhere is hungry or deprived or rejected or discriminated against. "Life to the full" is the desire of God for every person—anything less mars His image in us; it is the purpose of the resurrection.

Almost twenty years ago, Dr. Clarence Hall recounted this incident in a *Reader's Digest* article: "During the Easter season two years ago while I was in the Middle East, I met a man with the most triumphant spirit I have ever encountered. He was Abdul Mohammed, a waiter in a small inn near Bethlehem.

"Before the U. N. partition of Palestine he had been a successful merchant in the part of Jerusalem that now belongs to Israel. He was forced out and lost everything except his indomitable spirit. Now he performed his humble task with dignity."

On the evening before Easter Sunday Abdul took Dr. Hall out to Shepherd's Field—the scene of the angel's song. "Moonlight flooded the ancient hills, and in the distance a lamb bleated. Looking out toward the twinkling lights of Bethlehem, it was easy to transport oneself back 1900 years. After standing in silence for a while, Abdul said quietly, 'Many people say there's no guiding star these days for either Arabs or Israelis. They're wrong. *Stars are for those who look upward.* If we keep looking long enough in the right direction, a star will appear, and it will lead us, one day, to peace.' "

Then on Easter morning they went early to attend a sunrise service at the Garden Tomb. As they waited, Dr. Hall said impatiently, "Will the night never pass?" Abdul answered, "Never fear, my friend, the day will come, you cannot hold back the dawn."

Not now. Not ever. The revolution of faith cannot be held back; it is as sure as the resurrection of Christ.

Note: All Scripture references in this chapter are taken from *The New Testament of The Jerusalem Bible,* Doubleday and Company, Image Books, 1969.

MEET THE AUTHORS

The writers associated with me in *The Gift of Easter* are all talented Christian communicators. But of even greater importance to me, they are not merely persons of competence—colleagues in Christian service—but friends, some of many years while others are more recent.

Each, according to his gifts and convictions, views the miracle of Easter and the events leading up to it from varying perspectives. But all of them, as you have read, stand in awe before the most climactic Event in human history.

JOHN R. W. STOTT
Appointed Rector of All Souls, Langham Place, London in 1950 and served until September 1975 when he was appointed Rector Emeritus. He is immediate Past President of Scripture Union and Chairman of the Church of England Evangelical Council. Mr. Stott is the author of sixteen books, has conducted missions on a number of occasions in the Universities of Cambridge and Oxford and in various other British universities, as well as in universities in Canada, the United States, Australia, Africa, and Southeast Asia, and he travels extensively as a speaker at student and pastor's conferences.

Meet the Authors

RICHARD C. HALVERSON

Pastor of Fourth Presbyterian Church of Washington D.C. He has made over twenty separate trips to Asia and has visited every continent. His travels have included several around-the-world trips in the interest of training pastors and laymen working with problems of refugees, orphanages, and dispossessed people. One of the most interesting of his associations is with men in positions of national leadership who are providing direction to such activities in our country as the Presidential, Governors, and Mayors Prayer Breakfasts. Mr. Halverson is the author of seven books.

D. ELTON TRUEBLOOD

Professor-at-Large, Earlham College, where for twenty years before his retirement he was Professor of Philosophy. Prior to his tenure at Earlham, he was for nine years Professor of Philosophy of Religion at Stanford University. Elton Trueblood serves as President of Yokefellow Associates, is the author of twenty-eight books, and is in constant demand as a lecturer in the United States and abroad.

RAY C. STEDMAN

Pastor and founder of Peninsula Bible Church, Palo Alto, California, since 1950 where he emphasizes a strong laymen's training program and is presently developing an intern and pastor's training program called Discovery Center. As a speaker to pastor's conferences and ministering to missionaries, Mr. Stedman has traveled in Europe, the Orient, and

Central and South America. He is the author of nine books.

JOHN R. CLAYPOOL

Pastor of Broadway Baptist Church, Fort Worth, Texas, since 1971. Previous positions include a term of service as Pastor of Crescent Hill Baptist Church, Louisville, Kentucky. He has traveled under appointment to Japan and Israel, is a popular speaker at conferences and seminars, and is the author of one book.

DAVID POLING

Senior Minister, First Presbyterian Church of Albuquerque, New Mexico. He was Editor and President of *Christian Herald* from 1964 to 1971. Mr. Poling has a weekly syndicated newspaper column appearing in more than 600 papers in the United States and Canada and has featured articles in *The Reader's Digest, The Saturday Review, McCalls,* and *The New York Times.* He is the author of two books as well as several paperbacks.

CHARLES H. HUFFMAN

Rector, St. Matthew's Episcopal Church, Austin, Texas. Following a successful and rewarding career in business, Mr. Huffman received his divinity degree from the Seminary of the Southwest. Prior to his present appointment, he served as Assistant Rector of St. David's Episcopal Church, Austin, Texas, and as Associated Director of The Pittsburgh Experiment, Pittsburgh, Pennsylvania.

Meet the Authors

RAYMOND C. ORTLUND

Pastor, Lake Avenue Congregational Church, Pasadena, California. He ministers regularly to college and university groups for their Spiritual Emphasis Weeks, at Wycliffe Branch conferences, and three times has been the speaker at the Japan Keswick. Mr. Ortlund is the author of two books.

JOHN A. HUFFMAN, JR.

Senior Minister, First Presbyterian Church of Pittsburgh, Pennsylvania, a church with an impressive two hundred-year history—Mr. Huffman is the eleventh senior minister. His earlier appointments included that of Minister of Key Biscayne Presbyterian Church in Florida. He is the author of two books and has traveled internationally in thirty-five countries.

REUBEN JOB

A minister in the United Methodist Church, now serving as Associate General Secretary, Board of Discipleship, the United Methodist Church, Nashville, Tennessee. Mr. Job served as an air force chaplain during the Berlin crisis. Before assuming his present position he was Editor of Tidings and has written extensively for curriculum resources.

DAVID L. MCKENNA

President of Seattle Pacific College and a minister in the Free Methodist Church. Earlier positions include: Dean, Vice President, and Professor of Psychology of Spring Arbor College (Michigan), Assistant Professor in Higher Education at Ohio

State University and the University of Michigan; President of Spring Arbor College. He has served as Chairman of the Governor's Blue Ribbon Commission on Gambling for the State of Washington and is a Director of the American Association of Colleges.

RICHARD P. LANGFORD
Senior Minister, University Presbyterian Church, Seattle, Washington. He is a member of the Board of Trustees of Whitworth College and San Francisco Theological Seminary. Earlier appointments include twelve years with Young Life and as a minister at the First Presbyterian Church of Hollywood. He is active as a speaker at conferences and on seminary and university campuses.

GEORGE A. BUTTRICK
Recognized as one of the outstanding preachers of this century, he is held in high esteem by scholars as General Editor of *The Interpreter's Bible* and *The Interpreter's Dictionary of the Bible*. He now serves as visiting lecturer in homiletics at Louisville Presbyterian Seminary and Roble Lecturer in Christian Preaching at Southern Baptist Theological Seminary in Louisville.

CHARLIE W. SHEDD
Presbyterian minister, conference speaker, syndicated columnist, and author of more than a dozen books with sales of well over one million copies. Mr. Shedd is widely received as a radio and television personality, speaking to teenagers and adults on sex, marriage, and the family.

Meet the Authors

* * *

FLOYD THATCHER

Vice President of Word, Incorporated and Executive Editor of Word Books, Publisher, Waco, Texas. Former associations: Vice President, Publishing, Zondervan Publishing House; President, Cowman Publications, Inc. Writing credits include three earlier books, miscellaneous booklets and articles, and co-author with Charlie W. Shedd of the Christian Writers Seminar program on cassette tape.